MOVIE ★ ICONS

MAE WEST

EDITOR
PAUL DUNCAN

TEXT
DOMINIQUE MAINON & JAMES URSINI

PHOTOS
THE KOBAL COLLECTION

TASCHEN

HONG KONG KÖLN LONDON LOS ANGELES MADRID PARIS TOKYO

CONTENTS

1

MAE WEST: RISQUÉ BUSINESS

BY DOMINIQUE MAINON & JAMES URSINI

MAE WEST: FRECH GEWAGT

MAE WEST : LA SULFUREUSE

MAE WEST: RISQUÉ BUSINESS

by Dominique Mainon & James Ursini

In terms of celebrity icons, few attained the highest levels of fame and controversy as rapidly as Mae West. Labeled a "pornographer" by censorship boards, she was also one of 1930s Hollywood's most lucrative box-office draws (causing *Variety* in 1933 to label the star "as hot an issue as Hitler"). Nicknamed by critic George Jean Nathan "the Statue of Libido" and paid homage to in the title song of Cole Porter's musical *Anything Goes,* her voluptuous image and signature platinum blond hair became recognizable worldwide and for decades beyond her prime years of fame in the 1930s. In fact, even by the 1960s when the Beatles wanted to use her image on the cover of their *Sgt. Pepper's Lonely Hearts Club Band* album, those long-haired idols of a new generation were required to deliver a handwritten plea to the icon (which they dutifully did), since West herself always objected, as she said, to belonging to any "lonely hearts club."

Mae West's larger-than-life character is firmly entrenched in the realms of legend. Her imitators make frequent appearances in a variety of incarnations that both project and pantomime sex, as was her trademark. Celebrities (even animated cartoon characters such as Betty Boop) have mimicked Mae West's affected swagger, curvaceous figure and famously suggestive quips. "Sex is for her a cartoon which she delights in animating," claimed drama critic John Mason Brown. Never before did a woman act so brazenly carnal and sexually aggressive in theater and on screen — and become a star for it.

Beyond pure attitude, Mae West was an anomaly in several other areas. She was almost forty years old before gaining fame on screen. Her thick figure was almost matronly, even when adorned in tight sequined dresses and a myriad of jewels, in stark contrast to the young, slender and scarcely clad flappers that had risen to popularity in the late 1920s and early 1930s. Author Truman Capote once

PORTRAIT
Woman: "Goodness, what beautiful diamonds!" Mae West: "Goodness had nothing to do with it, dearie." / Frau: „Meine Güte, welch herrliche Diamanten!" Mae West: „Meine Güte hat damit nichts zu tun, Schätzchen." / Une femme : « Bonté divine ! Quels diamants magnifiques ! » Mae West : « Je ne vois pas ce que la bonté vient faire ici, Darling. »

"I generally avoid temptation unless I can't resist it."
Mae West

described Mae West as "the Big Ben of hourglass figures." Even furniture and objects have been imbued with her most memorable features. Surrealist Salvador Dalí designed a red silk sofa based upon the distinct shape of West's lips. And the famed "Mae West" inflatable life vest was named for its shapely form by the Allies in World War Two.

West was also notable for her daring. By 1926, Mae West had taken to writing her own risqué plays, and soon wrote herself into jail over obscenity charges for her daringly titled production, *Sex*. However, instead of backing down, West simply used the media attention to her advantage and soon followed up with yet another sexually charged and controversial play about homosexuality, titled *The Drag*. Her notoriety grew, as well as her pocketbook.

Receiving a motion picture contract with Paramount in 1932, Mae West was transported to a new level of fame. Though she had a relatively small part in her first film, *Night After Night*, leading man George Raft would later claim "she stole everything but the cameras." Her trademark wit combined with her daunting figure and well-coiffed blond hair would propel her to superstar status by the opening of her next film, *I'm No Angel* (1933), her biggest screen triumph and one of the films credited with bringing down the wrath of the Production Code Office, leading to a stricter enforcement of its puritanical code.

West's blatant and aggressive female sexuality, which she exposed on screen, was shocking in comparison with the more common portrayals of women as innocent coquettes or smoldering, sophisticated beauties. It was Mae West's rough girl charm, her "hooker with a heart of gold" attitude that won over men and women alike. Shuffling about with her exaggerated step and mischievous smile, she soon became an accomplished caricature of herself, particularly in later, tamer films such as *Belle of the Nineties* (1934), *Goin' To Town* (1935), and *My Little Chickadee* (1940) with W. C. Fields.

In comparison to other Hollywood celebrities of her day, Mae West was less prolific in her movie making. Yet she was no less powerful as an American icon, spawning a repertoire of fantastical stories about her past as well as the outlandish ways she maintained her eternal youth and her voracious appetite for men. As was her early life, her later personal life was always kept somewhat shrouded in a mystery of sequined gowns, huge hats, and bright polka-dotted ruffles. Like any good icon, she concentrated on the job of being an icon, keeping obscure who exactly was behind that larger-than-life figure.

ENDPAPERS/VOR- UND NACHSATZBLÄTTER/
PAGES DE GARDE
**PORTRAIT FOR 'SHE DONE HIM WRONG'
(1933)**

PAGES 2/3
STILL FROM 'MY LITTLE CHICKADEE' (1940)

PAGE 4
**PORTRAIT FOR 'EVERY DAY'S A HOLIDAY'
(1937)**

PAGES 6/7
PORTRAIT (1928)

PAGE 8
PORTRAIT

OPPOSITE /RECHTS /CI-CONTRE
PORTRAIT
Mae West: "When I'm good, I'm very good. But when I'm bad I'm better." / Mae West: „Wenn ich gut bin, dann bin ich sehr gut. Aber wenn ich schlimm bin, dann bin ich besser." / Mae West : « Quand je suis bonne, je suis très bonne. Mais quand je suis mauvaise, je suis encore meilleure. »

MAE WEST: FRECH GEWAGT

von Dominique Mainon & James Ursini

Kaum eine Filmikone war so rasch derart berühmt und zugleich so umstritten wie Mae West. Die Zensurbehörden beschimpften sie als „Pornografin", während sie in den dreißiger Jahren des vergangenen Jahrhunderts gleichzeitig zu den Kinostars gehörte, die die höchsten Einspielergebnisse brachten (was *Variety* 1933 zu dem Vergleich veranlasste, sie sei ein „ebenso heißes Thema wie Hitler"). Der Kritiker George Jean Nathan nannte sie „Freizügigkeitsstatue" („Statue of Libido"), und Cole Porter zollte ihr im Titelsong seines Musicals *Anything Goes* Tribut. Ihre üppigen Formen und ihr charakteristisches, platinblondes Haar waren der ganzen Welt ein Begriff — auch noch Jahrzehnte, nachdem sie den Höhepunkt ihrer Laufbahn überschritten hatte. Selbst in den sechziger Jahren noch, als die Beatles ihr Abbild für das Cover ihres Albums *Sgt. Pepper's Lonely Hearts Club Band* verwenden wollten, mussten diese langhaarigen Idole einer neuen Generation der Ikone einen handgeschriebenen Bettelbrief überbringen (was sie pflichtgemäß taten), weil West, wie sie selbst sagte, es stets abgelehnt habe, einem „Club der einsamen Herzen" anzugehören.

Mae Wests überlebensgroße Figur hat ihren festen Platz im Reich der Legende. Ihre Imitatoren greifen gern auf jenen mannigfaltigen Fundus an sexuellen Posen und Rollen zurück, der ihr Markenzeichen war. Viele Berühmtheiten (und selbst Zeichentrickfiguren wie Betty Boop) haben Mae Wests affektiertes Gewippe, ihre kurvenreiche Figur und ihre berühmten zweideutigen Sprüche nachgeahmt. „Sex ist für sie ein Cartoon, den sie mit Vergnügen animiert", behauptete der Kritiker John Mason Brown. Nie zuvor hat eine Frau auf Bühne und Leinwand Fleischeslust derart unverschämt offensiv zur Schau gestellt — und ist damit zum Star geworden.

Abgesehen von ihrer Geisteshaltung war Mae West auch auf einigen anderen Gebieten ein Phänomen. Sie war fast vierzig, bevor sie als Filmstar berühmt wurde. Ihre füllige Figur war beinahe matronenhaft, auch wenn sie in engen, paillettenbestickten Kleidern steckte und mit einer Unzahl von Juwelen geschmückt war — und stand im krassen Gegensatz zu jenen jungen, schlanken und spärlich bekleideten Backfischen der zwanziger und dreißiger Jahre, die dafür

PORTRAIT FOR 'I'M NO ANGEL' (1933)
Mae West [to Cary Grant]: "Oh, I'm very quick in a slow way." / Mae West [zu Cary Grant]: „Oh, ich bin sehr flott, auf langsame Art." / Mae West [à Cary Grant] : « Je suis très rapide … en y allant lentement. »

„Ich gehe der Versuchung normalerweise aus dem Weg, außer, wenn ich ihr nicht widerstehen kann."
Mae West

berühmt waren, sich über alle Konventionen hinwegzusetzen. Der Schriftsteller Truman Capote beschrieb Mae West einmal als den „Big Ben unter den Sanduhrfiguren". Selbst Möbel und andere Gegenstände wurden von ihren bekanntesten Merkmalen inspiriert. Der Surrealist Salvador Dalí entwarf ein rotes Seidensofa nach der unverkennbaren Form von Wests Lippen. Und die Alliierten im Zweiten Weltkrieg nannten ihre berühmte aufblasbare Rettungsweste „Mae West". Auch Wests Wagemut war bemerkenswert. Im Jahre 1926 hatte sie schon begonnen, ihre eigenen, anstößigen Theaterstücke zu schreiben und brachte sich mit ihrer kühn betitelten Produktion *Sex*, der man öffentliche Unzucht vorwarf, schon bald hinter Gitter. Statt sich aber kleinkriegen zu lassen, nutzte West die Aufmerksamkeit der Medien zu ihrem eigenen Vorteil und brachte schon bald ein weiteres kontroverses Stück mit dem Titel *The Drag* – diesmal zum Thema Homosexualität – auf die Bühne. Mit ihrem schlechten Ruf wuchs auch ihr Bankkonto.

Und mit einem Filmvertrag bei Paramount, 1932, erklomm Mae West eine ganz neue Stufe des Ruhms. Wenngleich sie in ihrem ersten Film *Night After Night* eine verhältnismäßig kleine Rolle spielte, behauptete ihr Filmpartner George Raft später, sie hätte allen die Schau gestohlen. Ihr typischer Witz in Verbindung mit ihrer beeindruckenden Figur und ihrem gestylten Blondschopf katapultierten sie in den Status eines Superstars, als ihr nächster Film – *Ich bin kein Engel*, (1933) – in die Kinos kam. Er war nicht nur ihr größter Triumph auf der Leinwand, sondern gilt auch als einer jener Filme, die den Grimm des Production Code Office weckten und dazu führten, dass die puritanischen Produktionsrichtlinien, die sich die Filmindustrie selbst auferlegt hatte, fortan strenger durchgesetzt wurden.

Wests auf der Leinwand offen zur Schau gestellte, aggressive weibliche Sexualität war im Vergleich mit der damals üblichen Darstellung von Frauen als unschuldig kokette oder elegant schmollende Schönheiten ein Schock. Mit ihrem derben Mädchencharme und ihrer Haltung als „Nutte mit goldenem Herzen" konnte Mae West Männer wie Frauen gleichermaßen für sich gewinnen. Ihr übertriebenes Stolzieren und ihr schelmisches Lächeln machten sie schon bald zu einer Karikatur ihrer selbst, insbesondere in späteren, zahmeren Filmen wie *Belle of the Nineties* (1934), *Goin' To Town* (1935) und *My Little Chickadee* (1940) mit W. C. Fields.

Im Vergleich zu anderen Hollywoodgrößen ihres Alters war Mae West in ihrer Filmkarriere weitaus weniger produktiv. Einflussreicher war sie als amerikanische Ikone, sie nährte einen breit gefächerten Fundus an phantastischen Geschichten über ihre Vergangenheit und über die ausgefallenen Methoden, mit denen sie ihre ewige Jugend und ihren unersättlichen Appetit auf Männer erhielt. Wie über ihren jungen Jahren lag auch über ihren späteren stets ein geheimnisvoller Schleier aus paillettenbesetzten Kleidern, großen Hüten und leuchtend getupften Rüschen. Wie es sich für eine gute Ikone ziemt, konzentrierte auch sie sich darauf, Ikone zu sein, und ließ im Ungewissen, wer wirklich hinter dieser überlebensgroßen Figur steckte.

PORTRAIT
Mae West: "Too much of a good thing ... can be wonderful." / Mae West: „Zuviel des Guten ... kann wunderbar sein." / Mae West : « Même quand c'est trop ... ça peut être divin. »

MAE WEST : LA SULFUREUSE

Dominique Mainon et James Ursini

Rares sont les célébrités qui ont atteint les sommets de la gloire et de la controverse aussi rapidement que Mae West. Qualifiée de « pornographe » par les commissions de censure, l'actrice est dans les années 1930 l'une des valeurs les plus sûres du box-office hollywoodien. (En 1933, *Variety* écrit que la star est un sujet « aussi brûlant que Hitler ».) Le critique George Jean Nathan la surnomme la « statue de la Libido », tandis que la chanson-titre de la comédie musicale *Anything Goes*, de Cole Porter, lui rend hommage. Ses formes voluptueuses et son incomparable chevelure bouclée blond platine sont bientôt connues dans le monde entier, une popularité qui s'étend bien au-delà de son apogée dans les années 1930. Ainsi, dans les années 1960, quand les Beatles veulent utiliser son image sur la pochette de leur album *Sergeant Pepper's Lonely Hearts Club Band*, Mae West exige des idoles aux cheveux longs de la nouvelle génération qu'ils lui envoient une lettre personnelle (ce dont ils s'acquittent consciencieusement), car elle s'est toujours refusée jusqu'à ce jour à figurer dans un quelconque « club des Cœurs solitaires ».

Personnalité plus grande que nature, Mae West est solidement enracinée dans le monde de la légende. Les spectacles d'imitation foisonnent de travestis parodiant ce sex-appeal qui constitue sa marque de fabrique. Des célébrités (jusqu'à des figures de dessins animés telle Betty Boop) copient la démarche chaloupée de la star, sa silhouette plantureuse et ses réparties percutantes. « Le sexe est un dessin qu'elle adore animer », déclare le critique de film John Mason Brown. Avant Mae West, jamais une femme n'avait conquis le statut de star en étalant sur les planches et à l'écran une telle débauche charnelle et une telle assurance sexuelle.

Au-delà de l'image qu'elle s'est créée, Mae West se singularise en plusieurs points. Elle a près de quarante ans quand elle connaît la gloire au cinéma ; dotée de rondeurs généreuses, elle fait presque matrone malgré ses robes à paillettes moulées au corps et ses montagnes de bijoux ; elle est l'antithèse des garçonnes sveltes, aux tenues légères, qui imposent leur style au tournant des années 1920-1930. L'écrivain Truman Capote la compare à un « Big Ben à la silhouette en

PORTRAIT FOR 'I'M NO ANGEL' (1933)
Mae West: "You can say what you like about long dresses, but they cover a multitude of shins." / Mae West: „Über lange Kleider kann man sagen, was man will, aber sie verdecken vieles — auch viele Sünden." / Mae West : « Qu'on aime ou non les robes longues, elles couvrent là où il faut. »

« Normalement, j'évite la tentation, jusqu'à ce que je n'y résiste plus. »
Mae West

sablier». Des meubles et tant d'autres objets évoquent ses attributs les plus mémorables. Le peintre surréaliste Salvador Dalí crée ainsi un sofa de soie rouge d'après la forme unique des lèvres de Mae West. Durant la Seconde Guerre mondiale, les Alliés baptisent le célèbre gilet de sauvetage gonflable «Mae West» en référence aux formes généreuses de la star.

L'audace de Mae West est notoire. Dès 1926, elle écrit ses propres pièces de théâtre sulfureuses, une entreprise qui lui vaut de se retrouver en prison, inculpée d'obscénité pour sa production au titre provocant, *Sex*. Or, loin de se rétracter, elle tire parti de la publicité que lui font les médias et récidive bientôt avec *The Drag*, une autre pièce aussi chaude que controversée, qui aborde le thème de l'homosexualité. Sa notoriété croît, de même que son compte en banque.

Après ses débuts au cinéma à la Paramount en 1932, Mae West se retrouve dans la cour des grands. Elle n'a pourtant qu'un rôle modeste dans son premier film, *Nuit après nuit*, au côté de la star masculine George Raft, qui dira d'elle plus tard : «Elle s'est tout approprié, sauf le matériel de tournage.» Le mélange d'ironie, de verbe haut et de volupté blond platine exsudant la sensualité propulse Mae West au rang de superstar après la première de son second film *Je ne suis pas un ange* (1933), qui sera son plus grand triomphe à l'écran. Ce film attire vite les foudres du Production Code Office, qui s'empresse de renforcer son code puritain.

Bombe sexuelle crevant l'écran, Mae West ne peut que choquer face aux personnages féminins de l'époque, ingénues minaudières ou beautés sophistiquées aguicheuses. Le charme brut de Mae, son côté «fille au cœur d'or» lui valent autant l'affection des hommes que des femmes. Accentuant sa célèbre démarche chaloupée, le sourire déluré, elle devient bientôt sa propre parodie parfaite, notamment dans ses films ultérieurs, plus sages, tels *Ce n'est pas un péché* (1934), *Je veux être une lady* (1935) et *Mon petit poussin chéri* (1940) avec W. C. Fields.

Comparée aux autres célébrités hollywoodiennes de son temps, Mae West a eu une carrière cinématographique moins prolifique. Pourtant, son image d'icône américaine est tout aussi puissante, engendrant tout un répertoire d'histoires fantaisistes sur son passé, sur les recettes secrètes de sa jeunesse éternelle et sur son appétit vorace de la gent masculine. De même qu'à l'époque de sa jeunesse, sa vie privée dans ses dernières années reste entourée d'une aura de mystère — une vie dissimulée sous des robes à sequins, des volants à pois et d'immenses capelines. Comme toute célébrité du 7e art qui se respecte, Mae West se concentre sur son rôle de star, maintenant dans l'ombre la face cachée de son personnage plus grand que nature.

PAGE 22
PORTRAIT (CIRCA 1915)
West was a successful vamp and vaudevillian playing venues in New York and Chicago. She would sing and do a suggestive shimmy dance. / West war als Vamp und Varietékünstlerin auf den Bühnen von New York und Chicago erfolgreich. Beim Singen legte sie einen recht suggestiven Shimmy aufs Parkett. / Mae West, vamp et comédienne de vaudeville à succès, joue dans les théâtres de New York et Chicago. Elle chante et contribue au lancement du *shimmy*, une danse érotique.

PORTRAIT FOR 'NIGHT AFTER NIGHT' (1932)
Mae West: "I never worry about diets. The only carrots that interest me are the number you get in a diamond." / Mae West: „Ich mache mir nie Gedanken über Diäten. / Mae West : «Je me fiche des régimes. Je préfère croquer des diamants plutôt que des carottes.»

2

VISUAL FILMOGRAPHY

FILMOGRAFIE IN BILDERN

FILMOGRAPHIE EN IMAGES

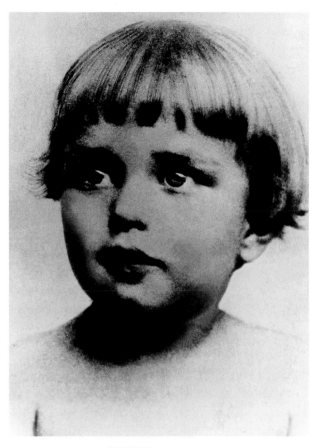

PORTRAIT
Baby West, an actress at age four. / Baby West, schon mit vier eine Schauspielerin. / Baby West débute sa carrière à quatre ans.

PORTRAIT FOR THE PLAY 'THE MIMIC WORLD' (1921)
The actress played on Broadway in a revue for the Schubert brothers. Her shimmy dance was described "as if it were an attempt to get out of a straight-jacket without the use of the hands." / Am Broadway trat die Sängerin in einer Revue der Brüder Schubert (Theater-manager) auf. Man schrieb, ihr Shimmy gleiche einem „Versuch, sich ohne Gebrauch der Hände aus einer Zwangsjacke zu befreien". / À Broadway, Mae joue dans un spectacle aux côtés des frères Schubert. Sa façon de danser le *shimmy* faisait penser à quelqu'un « qui essaie de sortir d'une camisole de force sans se servir des mains ».

MAE WEST IN COURT (1926)
West in court during her trial for "public obscenity"
as a result of her transgressive play 'Sex.' Mae West:
"I believe in censorship. I made a fortune out of it." /
West wegen öffentlicher Unzucht vor Gericht, weil sie
mit ihrem Theaterstück Sex gegen die „guten Sitten"
verstoßen hatte. Mae West: „Ich glaube an die Zensur.
Ich habe damit ein Vermögen gemacht." / « Au
tribunal » : Mae West est inculpée d'« obscénité
publique » pour Sex, sa pièce provocante. Mae
West : « Je suis pour la censure ; elle m'a rapporté une
fortune. »

MAE WEST VISITS JAIL
She turned a serious conviction (she served eight days)
into a glamorous and ironic moment as she lords it over
her obviously enamored jailer. / „Stippvisite im Gefängnis": Die Haftstrafe, von der sie acht Tage absaß,
verwandelte sie in ein glamouröses Spektakel – ihren
offenbar faszinierten Gefängniswärter scheint sie voll
im Griff zu haben. / « Visite en prison » : condamnée à
huit jours de détention, Mae West ne perd rien de sa
superbe et de son ironie, toisant son geôlier visiblement
énamouré d'un air pour le moins glamour.

PORTRAIT (1928)

The actress luxuriating in her exotic swan bed, an iconic image for West. She gave the impression of spontaneous quips but she was a hardworking writer as well as a performer. / Die Schauspielerin aalt sich in ihrem exotischen Schwanenbett — eine typische West-Pose. Ihre frechen Bonmots erweckten stets den Eindruck von spontaner Leichtigkeit, aber sie arbeitete hart, sowohl als Schriftstellerin als auch als Schauspielerin. / Image d'une icône : Mae West se prélasse dans son lit-cygne exotique. Derrière son verbe haut qui paraît spontané se cache une comédienne et scénariste âpre à la tâche.

"I've been rich and I've been poor ... Believe me, rich is better."
Mae West

„Ich war reich, und ich war arm ... Glauben Sie mir: reich ist besser."
Mae West

SCREEN TEST

One of many screen tests West endured in order to break into Hollywood. Mae West: "Give a man a free hand and he'll run it all over you." / Einer von vielen Leinwandtests, die West über sich ergehen ließ, um endlich in Hollywood Fuß zu fassen. Mae West: „Gib einem Mann freie Hand, dann wirst Du sie bald an Deinem ganzen Körper spüren." / Un des nombreux bouts d'essai endurés avant de conquérir Hollywood. Mae West : « Laissez les mains libres à un homme, et elles se baladeront partout sur vous. »

« J'ai été riche et pauvre … Croyez-moi, il vaut mieux être riche. »
Mae West

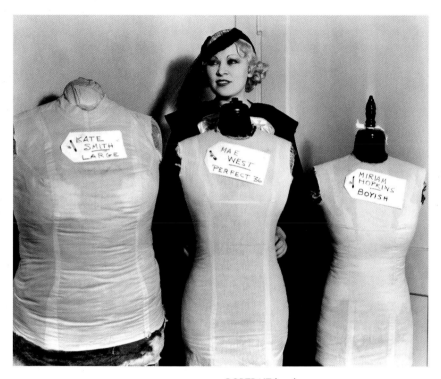

PORTRAIT (1932)
Smaller than Kate Smith but larger than Miriam
Hopkins, a voluptuous West. / Kleiner als Kate Smith,
aber größer als Miriam Hopkins: eine üppige West. /
Plus petite que Kate Smith mais plus grande que Miriam
Hopkins : une Mae West voluptueuse.

PORTRAIT FOR 'NIGHT AFTER NIGHT' (1932)
West strikes a pose, a little Harlow but a lot of West.
Mae West: "It is better to be looked over than
overlooked." / West posiert: ein bisschen Harlow, aber
ganz viel West. Mae West: „Es ist besser, gemustert zu
werden, als ausgemustert." / Mae West prend la pose :
un peu de Jean Harlow, beaucoup de West. Mae West :
« Il vaut mieux attirer les regards plutôt qu'être
regardée sans attirer. »

PORTRAIT FOR 'NIGHT AFTER NIGHT' (1932)
Lifelong friends, West and George Raft were reputedly
lovers when he was a runner picking up 'Diamond Lil'
profits for gangster Owen Madden. They died within a
few days of each other. / West und George Raft waren
nicht nur ein Leben lang Freunde, sondern angeblich
auch ein Liebespaar, als er noch für den Gangster Owen
Madden Schutzgelder aus den Gewinnen kassierte, die
Diamond Lil abwarf. Raft starb nur zwei Tage nach ihr. /
Liés par une amitié indéfectible, on a prêté une liaison
à Mae West et George Raft lorsque ce dernier était un
coursier rapportant les recettes de *Diamond Lil* au
racketteur Owen Madden. Ils disparaîtront à quelques
jours d'écart.

ADVERT FOR 'NIGHT AFTER NIGHT' (1932)

Raft Zooms to Stardom in Knockout Picture!

with

GEORGE RAFT
CONSTANCE CUMMINGS
WYNNE GIBSON
MAE WEST
ALISON SKIPWORTH

Directed by Archie Mayo
From a story by Louis Bromfield

Says *"Hollywood Reporter"*:

"Order Big Letters to Spell Out His Name 'GEORGE RAFT' in 'Night After Night' . . . He is *THE* Picture...With Great Entertainment To Back Him Up...And, The One and Only Mae West In Her First Screen Appearance . . . She's A Riot . . . Constance Cummings, At Her Best. . . . A SWELL PICTURE!"

NIGHT *after* NIGHT

A Paramount Picture

STILL FROM 'NIGHT AFTER NIGHT' (1932)
West rewrote her part because she found it colorless,
to the chagrin of the director but the delight of the
studio. / Dass West ihre Rolle umschrieb, weil sie ihr zu
farblos erschien, ärgerte den Regisseur, erfreute aber
das Studio. / Mae West réécrit son rôle, qu'elle trouve
trop plat ; le réalisateur est ennuyé, mais le producteur
enchanté.

STILL FROM 'NIGHT AFTER NIGHT' (1932)
Surrounded by adoring men, an image which West will
repeat throughout her career both on stage and screen.
Mae West: "I only have 'yes' men around me. Who
needs 'no' men?" / Von Bewunderern umringt — ein Bild,
das sich in Wests Theater- und Filmkarriere stetig
wiederholte. Mae West: „Ich bin nur von Jasagern
umgeben. Wer braucht denn schon Neinsager?" /
Entourée d'une cour d'hommes, une image qui
accompagnera Mae West tout au long de sa vie
professionnelle. Mae West : « Je n'ai que des hommes
qui disent "oui" autour de moi. Pourquoi devrait-on
préférer ceux qui disent "non" ? »

STILL FROM 'NIGHT AFTER NIGHT' (1932)
As Raft's wise and sexy ex-mistress she radiates the
charisma which would soon make her a star. / Als Joes
(Raft) kluge und erotische Ex-Freundin strahlt sie ein
Charisma aus, das sie bald zum Star machen sollte. /
Intelligente et sexy, l'ex-maîtresse de Raft a acquis un
charisme qui fera bientôt d'elle une star.

"Good sex is like good bridge. If you don't have a
good partner, you'd better have a good hand."
Mae West

„Guter Sex ist wie gutes Bridge. Wenn man schon
keinen guten Partner hat, dann sollte man
wenigstens eine gute Hand haben."
Mae West

« Bien faire l'amour, c'est comme bien jouer au
bridge. Sans bon partenaire, mieux vaut avoir une
bonne main. »
Mae West

STILL FROM 'NIGHT AFTER NIGHT' (1932)
With comic co-star Alison Skipworth, West camps it
up. / Mit der Komödiantin Alison Skipworth an ihrer
Seite haut West mächtig auf den Putz. / Mae West fait
la belle aux côtés de la comédienne Alison Skipworth.

PAGES 38/39
**ON THE SET OF 'SHE DONE HIM WRONG'
(1933)**
Here director Lowell Sherman, who as a silent film actor
starred in D. W. Griffith's 'Way Down East,' collaborates
with West on the set. / Hier berät sich Regisseur Lowell
Sherman, der als Schauspieler schon in D. W. Griffiths
Stummfilm *Weit im Osten* aufgetreten war, während der
Dreharbeiten mit West. / Mae West et le réalisateur
Lowell Sherman, acteur du cinéma muet qui joua dans
À travers l'orage de D. W. Griffith.

STILL FROM 'SHE DONE HIM WRONG' (1933)
Paramount under new leadership takes a chance on West's controversial play 'Diamond Lil.' Here she allows Gilbert Roland to admire her. / Unter neuer Leitung geht Paramount das Risiko ein, Wests umstrittenes Stück *Diamond Lil* zu verfilmen. Hier gestattet sie Gilbert Roland, sie zu bewundern. / La nouvelle direction de la Paramount prend le risque de tourner la pièce controversée *Diamond Lil* écrite par Mae West. Ici, elle se laisse admirer par Gilbert Roland.

STILL FROM 'SHE DONE HIM WRONG' (1933)
The film was a huge success, costing $200,000 but returning $2.2 million, and helped pull Paramount out of the financial red. Noah Beery plays Gus Jordan, who keeps Lady Lou in diamonds. / Der Film kostete 200.000 Dollar und spielte 2,2 Millionen ein. Dieser gewaltige Erfolg half Paramount, aus den roten Zahlen herauszukommen. Noah Beery spielt Gus Jordan, der dafür sorgt, dass Lady Lou die Diamanten nicht ausgehen. / Succès énorme, le film qui a coûté 200 000 dollars en rapporte 2,2 millions et sort la Paramount de ses ennuis financiers. Noah Beery joue Gus Jordan couvrant Lady Lou de diamants.

STILL FROM 'SHE DONE HIM WRONG' (1933)
West spied Cary Grant on the set. Informed he was an
extra, she said, "If he can't talk, I'll take him." / West
erspähte Cary Grant am Set. Als man ihr mitteilte, er sei
ein Komparse, antwortete sie: „Wenn er nicht reden
kann, nehme ich ihn." / Apercevant Cary Grant sur le
plateau, Mae West apprend qu'il est figurant. Elle dit:
« Je le prends s'il ne sait pas causer. »

**PORTRAIT FOR 'SHE DONE HIM WRONG'
(1933)**
West caused the Hays Office sleepless nights, not only
with this film but with portraits like this. / West
bereitete den Zensoren schlaflose Nächte – nicht nur
mit diesem Film, sondern auch mit Porträts wie
diesem. / Avec ce film, et des portraits de ce genre,
Mae West causera bien des nuits d'insomnie aux
censeurs du Hays Office.

STILL FROM 'SHE DONE HIM WRONG' (1933)
When West sang 'Easy Rider,' it was the first time that
authentic blues was featured in a mainstream
Hollywood film. / Wests Darbietung des Lieds „Easy
Rider" war die erste echte Bluesnummer, die in einem
großen Hollywood-Film zu hören war. / Mae West
chante «Easy Rider»: c'est la première fois qu'un blues
authentique est interprété dans un film hollywoodien.

PAGES 46/47
STILL FROM 'SHE DONE HIM WRONG' (1933)
Although many believe that West 'discovered' Grant, he
had already appeared in 8 other films, including 'Blonde
Venus' with Marlene Dietrich. / Viele glauben, West
habe Grant „entdeckt", aber er hatte bereits zuvor in
acht Filmen mitgespielt, darunter *Blonde Venus*. / Gary
Grant a joué dans huit films dont *Vénus Blonde* avant
d'être «découvert» par Mae West.

ON THE SET OF 'SHE DONE HIM WRONG'
(1933)
Filming started on 14 November 1932, continued until
the end of December, then the film was released in
February 1933. / Die Dreharbeiten begannen am 14.
November 1932 und zogen sich bis Ende Dezember. Im
Februar 1933 kam der Film dann in die Kinos. / Le film
arrive dans les salles en février 1933 après le tournage
qui a duré du 14 novembre à fin décembre 1932.

*"I'm the lady who works at Paramount all day ...
and Fox all night."*
Mae West

„*Ich bin die Dame, die den ganzen Tag für
Paramount arbeitet ... und die ganze Nacht für
‚Fox' [‚Fox'/‚fucks' = ‚die ganze Nacht vögelt]."*
Mae West

« *Je suis la dame qui travaille chez Paramount
toute la journée ... et Fox ["Fox"/"fucks" = "qui b ..."]
toute la nuit.* »
Mae West

STILL FROM 'SHE DONE HIM WRONG' (1933)
Under threat from a jealous Russian Rita (Rafaela
Ottiano). / Hier wird sie von der eifersüchtigen „Russian
Rita" (Rafaela Ottiano) bedroht. / Menacée par une
Russe jalouse (Rafaela Ottiano).

STILL FROM 'SHE DONE HIM WRONG' (1933)
Spurned lover Chick Clark (Owen Moore) escapes from
jail to kill his "faithless" Lady Lou … / Der verschmähte
Liebhaber Chick Clark (Owen Moore) bricht aus dem
Gefängnis aus, um seine „treulose" Lady Lou umzu-
bringen … / L'amant délaissé Chick Clark (Owen Moore)
s'est enfui de prison pour tuer sa Lady Lou volage …

STILL FROM 'SHE DONE HIM WRONG' (1933)
… but such is the power of his love for her that he
cannot go through with it. Mae West: "Love conquers all
things except poverty and toothache." / … aber seine
Liebe zu ihr ist so stark, dass er seinen Plan nicht in
die Tat umzusetzen vermag. Mae West: „Die Liebe
überwindet alles … außer Armut und Zahnschmerzen." /
… mais il l'aime trop pour passer à l'acte. Mae West:
«L'amour a raison de tout, sauf de la pauvreté et des
rages de dents.»

STILL FROM 'SHE DONE HIM WRONG' (1933)
Almost forty years old by the time she is a star,
West displays her ample charms with good natured
sexuality. / Sie ist fast vierzig, als sie ein Star wird,
und sie stellt ihre zahlreichen Reize mit einer un-
gezwungenen Natürlichkeit zur Schau. / À près de
quarante ans, la star exhibe ses charmes plantureux
avec un naturel déconcertant.

*"I'll try anything once, twice if I like it, three times
to make sure."*
Mae West

*„Ich probiere alles einmal aus; zweimal, wenn's mir
gefällt; dreimal, um sicher zu sein."*
Mae West

*« J'essaie tout une fois, deux fois si j'aime bien, trois
fois pour être sûre. »*
Mae West

STILL FROM 'SHE DONE HIM WRONG' (1933)
Men like she wants them, "guns" erect. / So mag sie die
Männer: mit erigierten „Kanonen". / Des hommes
comme elle les aime, prêts à «tirer des coups».

PAGES 54/55
ADVERT FOR 'I'M NO ANGEL' (1933)
Mae West: "Virtue has its own reward, but no sale at the
box office." / Mae West: „Tugend wird belohnt, aber
nicht mit guten Einspielergebnissen." / Mae West:
«La vertu est certainement payante, mais pas au box-
office.»

Mae West Gives!

"Yes", says Mae, "I've got to hand it to them!"

 "MY LIPS to those 786 exhibitors who played PARAMOUNT'S 'She Done Him Wrong' twice. You've got me, boys."

 "MY GOOD RIGHT ARM to the 108 fine showmen who played PARAMOUNT'S 'She Done Him Wrong' three times and to those 28 boys who played it four times. I go for them in a big way."

 "MY DIAMOND STUDDED GARTER to those 7 boys who played PARAMOUNT'S 'She Done Him Wrong' five times, to the 6 exhibitors who played it six times and to the 2 who played it seven times. It's got to be *intimate* for men like that."

 "MY OWN PERSONAL INVITATION to that outstanding exhibitor who played PARAMOUNT'S 'She Done Him Wrong' 10 times. *He fascinates me.*"

WHO SAI

HERE ISN'T ANY MORE...

Heaven's ahead for the boys who fly high with "I'M NO ANGEL"

*"I'M NO ANGEL" ADVERTISING PRIZE. For the guy who puts on the best advertising campaign on "I'm No Angel", (based on the material available in the "I'm No Angel" press book) I offer a personally conducted *"Come Up and See Me Some time"* trip—a round-trip ticket to Hollywood with expenses for one week.

"I'M NO ANGEL" RE-BOOKING PRIZES. To every good showman who replays "I'm No Angel", I will send a specially auto-graphed copy of my new book, "HOW TO MISBEHAVE"

"I'M NO ANGEL" GRAND PRIZE. As my personal present to the good man who plays "I'm No Angel" the greatest number of times, I give a diamond-studded watch with an intimate inscription in the back. It's got to be good for a man like that!"

C'mon boys, spread your wings with me in "I'm No Angel"

Mae West

* Contest starts October 6th . . . ends January 1st
In case of tie duplicate prizes will be awarded
Send all entries to the "I'm No Angel" Advertising Campaign Contest **to R. M. Gillham, Room 1202 Paramount Building, New York City**

"I'm No Angel"... says MAE WEST! "but I've spread my wings a bit...
there're people who've been places and seen things... but I've been things and seen places."

PARAMOUNT *Presents* MAE WEST in "I'M NO ANGEL"
with CARY GRANT. Directed by WESLEY RUGGLES

STILL FROM 'I'M NO ANGEL' (1933)
Under further pressure from the Hays Office,
Paramount and West soften the sexuality and cynicism
of the main character. / Auf weiteren Druck durch die
Zensur dämpfen Paramount und West die Sexualität
und den Zynismus der Hauptfigur. / Sous la pression du
Hays Office, Paramount et Mae West réduisent le sex-
appeal et le cynisme de l'héroïne.

PAGES 58/59
STILL FROM 'I'M NO ANGEL' (1933)
West belts out 'They Call Me Sister Honky Tonk' in the
robust, carnal style she made her trademark. / West
brüllt „They Call Me Sister Honky Tonk" in der derb-
sinnlichen Art, die sie zu ihrem Markenzeichen
machte. / West entonne « They Call Me Sister Honky
Tonk » avec la sensualité gouailleuse qui est sa marque
de fabrique.

ADVERT FOR 'I'M NO ANGEL' (1933)

STILL FROM 'I'M NO ANGEL' (1933)
Tira (Mae West) breaks up with Slick Wiley (Ralf
Harolde) when he goes too far rolling a mark. / Tira
(Mae West) trennt sich von Slick Wiley (Ralf Harolde),
als er beim Würfelspiel zu weit geht. / Tira (Mae West)
rompt avec Slick Wiley (Ralf Harolde) qui a dépassé les
limites.

"A man has one hundred dollars and you leave him
with two dollars, that's subtraction."
Mae West

„Ein Mann hat hundert Dollar, und Du lässt ihm
zwei. Das nennt man Subtraktion."
Mae West

« Un homme a cent dollars, vous lui en laissez deux,
ça s'appelle une soustraction. »
Mae West

STILL FROM 'I'M NO ANGEL' (1933)
Before photos of ex-lovers, including an African-American, quite a daring gibe at Hollywood racism of the period. Mae West: "It's not the men in my life that count, it's the life in my men." / Vor Fotos ihrer früheren Liebhaber, darunter auch ein Schwarzer – ein sehr gewagter Seitenhieb bei dem damals in Hollywood vorherrschenden Rassismus. Mae West: „Es sind nicht die Männer in meinem Leben, die zählen, sondern es ist das Leben in meinen Männern." / Devant des photos d'ex-amants, dont un Afro-Américain, un véritable défi au racisme hollywoodien de l'époque. Mae West : « Ce ne sont pas les hommes dans ma vie qui comptent, mais la vie dans mes hommes. »

PAGES 62/63
STILL FROM 'I'M NO ANGEL' (1933)
Filmed from July to September 1933, it went on to gross $2.3 million. / Der Film wurde zwischen Juli und September 1933 gedreht und spielte 2,3 Millionen Dollar ein. / Tourné de juillet à septembre 1933, le film rapporte 2,3 millions de dollars.

STILL FROM 'I'M NO ANGEL' (1933)
West not only tames men but animals as well. Tira's act
is a sensation because she puts her head into the lion's
mouth. / West bändigt nicht nur Männer, sondern auch
Tiere. Tiras Nummer ist eine Sensation, weil sie ihren
Kopf in das Maul des Löwen steckt. / Une dompteuse
d'hommes et d'animaux. Dans une scène impres-
sionnante, Tira met sa tête dans la gueule du lion.

ON THE SET OF 'I'M NO ANGEL' (1933)
Since she was a little girl, West dreamed of being a lion
tamer, so it was a thrill for her to work with a real one. /
Weil West schon als kleines Mädchen davon geträumt
hatte, Löwenbändigerin zu werden, war es für sie
aufregend, mit einer echten Wildkatze zu arbeiten. /
Toute petite, Mae rêvait déjà d'être dompteuse de lions.
Elle adore travailler avec un vrai fauve.

She takes **GRANT**

Like **GRANT** took **RICHMOND**

MAE WEST in "I'M NO ANGE[L]
with CARY GRAN[T]
directed by Wesley Ruggle[s]

if it's a PARAMOUNT PICTURE, it's the best show in tow[n]

LOBBY CARD FOR 'I'M NO ANGEL' (1933)
Mae West: "Anything worth doing is worth doing
slowly." / Mae West: „Alles, was wert ist, gemacht zu
werden, ist es wert, langsam gemacht zu werden." /
Mae West : « Quand ça vaut la peine, il faut y aller
lentement. »

ADVERT FOR 'I'M NO ANGEL' (1933)
Mae West: "A man's kiss is his signature." / Mae West:
„Der Kuss eines Mannes ist seine Unterschrift." / Mae
West : « Le baiser d'un homme est sa signature. »

STILL FROM 'I'M NO ANGEL' (1933)
Nobody messes with Mae West: Tira sues her ex-lover
for breach of promise. / Mit Mae West legt man sich
besser nicht an: Tira verklagt ihren Ex-Liebhaber, weil
er das Eheversprechen gebrochen hatte. / On ne se
moque pas de Mae West : Tira poursuit son ex-amant
pour rupture de fiançailles.

*"It's not what I do, but the way I do it. It's not what I
say, but the way I say it."*
Mae West

*„Es ist nicht das, was ich tue, sondern wie ich es
tue. Es ist nicht das, was ich sage, sondern wie ich
es sage."*
Mae West

*« Ce n'est pas ce que je fais, mais ma façon de le
faire, ce n'est pas ce que je dis, mais ma façon de le
dire. »*
Mae West

STILL FROM 'I'M NO ANGEL' (1933)
Although Grant was not discovered by West, it is fair to
say that she was responsible for his rise to stardom. /
Auch wenn Grant nicht von West entdeckt wurde, kann
man doch behaupten, dass sie für seinen Aufstieg zum
Star verantwortlich war. / Mae West n'a pas découvert
Gary Grant, mais il est devenu une star grâce à elle.

PAGES 70 & 71
**ADVERTS FOR 'BELLE OF THE NINETIES'
(1934)**
Originally titled 'It Ain't No Sin,' the title was not the
only thing to be censored by the new, tough regime of
Joseph Breen in the Production Code Office. / Bei dem
Film, der ursprünglich *It Ain't No Sin* heißen sollte, war
der Titel nicht das einzige, was der Zensur durch den
knallharten neuen Oberzensor Joseph Breen zum
Opfer fiel. / Sous le nouveau régime implacable de
Joseph Breen, le Production Code Office ne censure
pas seulement le titre du film *Ce n'est pas un péché*.

Love is the sweetest thing

Adolph Zukor presents **MAE WEST** in "IT AIN'T NO SIN" with Roger Pryor
John Mack Brown · Duke Ellington & Band · A Paramount Picture · Directed by Leo McCarey

Rough
DIAMONDS IN
THE MAKING

Holph Zukor presents **MAE WEST** in "IT AIN'T NO SIN" with Roger Pryor
hn Mack Brown · Duke Ellington & Band · A Paramount Picture · Directed by Leo McCarey

Tall, dark and handsome

Adolph Zukor prese

MAE WES

in

"IT AIN'T NO S

with Roger Pry
John Mack Brov
Duke Ellington a
his famous orches

A Paramount Pict
Directed by Leo McCa

ADVERT FOR 'BELLE OF THE NINETIES' (1934)
Producer Emanuel Cohen decided to submit an
outrageous version of the script to the Production
Code, so that the compromises were close to what he
wanted. / Produzent Emanuel Cohen legte der Zensur
eine Drehbuchfassung vor, die so unverschämt war, dass
die Kompromisse dann ungefähr dem entsprachen, was
er ursprünglich im Sinn hatte. / Le producteur Emanuel
Cohen soumet un scénario outrageux du film au
Production Code, et obtient les compromis escomptés.

PAGES 75 & 76
**COSTUME SKETCHES FOR 'BELLE OF THE
NINETIES' (1934)**
Legendary costume designer Travis Banton also worked
with Mae West on 'Goin' to Town.' / Der Kostümbildner
Travis Banton arbeitete bei Goin' to Town mit Mae West. /
Le légendaire Travis Banton a dessiné les costumes de
Mae West pour Je veux être une lady.

POSTER FOR 'BELLE OF THE NINETIES' (1934)

PAGES 74 & 77
STILLS FROM 'BELLE OF THE NINETIES' (1934)
In a time when figures were sleeker à la Harlow, West
defied the standard of female beauty, and proved that
women moving into middle age could be sexy and
desirable. / In einer Zeit, in der schlanke Formen à la
Harlow ‚in' waren, stellte West die weiblichen
Schönheitsideale auf den Kopf und bewies, dass Frauen
in den mittleren Jahren durchaus sexy und
begehrenswert sein konnten. / Défiant les critères de
beauté gracile à la Harlow de l'époque, Mae West
prouve que les femmes matures sont encore sexy et
désirables.

STILL FROM 'BELLE OF THE NINETIES' (1934)
Ruby Carter (Mae West), beauty queen of the nightclub
world, gives up her lover, prizefighter Tiger Kid (Roger
Pryor), so that he can have a chance of becoming the
champion. / Ruby Carter (Mae West), Schönheits-
königin aus der Welt der Nachtclubs, verzichtet auf
ihren Liebhaber, den Preisboxer Tiger Kid (Roger
Pryor), damit er eine Chance bekommt, den Meister-
titel zu gewinnen. / Ruby Carter (Mae West), reine des
night-clubs, renonce à son amant, le boxeur Tiger Kid
(Roger Pryor), pour ne pas mettre sa carrière de
champion en péril.

"A hard man is good to find."
Mae West

„Einen harten Mann zu finden, ist gute Arbeit."
Mae West

« Ça fait du bien de trouver un homme fort. »
Mae West

STILL FROM 'BELLE OF THE NINETIES' (1934)
Every good turn turns bad, and Ruby ends up embroiled
in the illegal schemes of Ace Lamont (John Miljan). /
Alles Gute wendet sich zum Schlechten, und am Ende
ist Ruby in die illegalen Machenschaften von Ace
Lamont (John Miljan) verstrickt. / Poursuivie par la
malchance, Ruby se retrouve mêlée aux machinations
d'Ace Lamont (John Miljan).

STILL FROM 'BELLE OF THE NINETIES' (1934)
West insisted on using Duke Ellington and his band for
her number, 'He Was Her Man, But He Came to See Me
Sometime.' / West bestand darauf, Duke Ellington und
seine Band bei ihrer Nummer „He Was Her Man, but He
Came to See Me Sometime" spielen zu lassen. / West a
imposé Duke Ellington et son orchestre pour se faire
accompagner dans son numéro « He Was Her Man, But
He Came to See Me Sometime » (« C'était son homme,
mais il venait me voir de temps à autre »).

**PORTRAIT FOR 'BELLE OF THE NINETIES'
(1934)**
The period gowns, hats and overall sheen of the
production belie the melancholy tone of West's songs
and character. / Die zeitgenössischen Kostüme und
Hüte sowie der allgemeine Glanz der Produktion
passen weder zum melancholischen Ton der Lieder,
die West singt, noch zur Figur, die sie darstellt. / Robes
d'époque, chapeaux à plumes et décor flamboyant
s'opposent au personnage et aux chansons
mélancoliques de Mae West.

ON THE SET OF 'BELLE OF THE NINETIES' (1934)

In West's plays and films, she demonstrated a sisterly solidarity with a succession of African-American maids. Here she is with Libby Taylor, her maid onscreen and in life. / In ihren Stücken und Filmen demonstrierte West eine schwesterliche Solidarität mit einer Reihe dunkelhäutiger Dienstmädchen. Hier ist sie mit Libby Taylor zu sehen, die sowohl im Leben als auch auf der Leinwand ihr Dienstmädchen war. / Sur les planches et à l'écran, Mae manifeste une solidarité fraternelle avec ses bonnes afro-américaines. On la voit ici avec Libby Taylor, sa femme de chambre dans le film comme dans la vie.

PORTRAIT FOR 'BELLE OF THE NINETIES' (1934)

In 1934, Mae West was the highest-paid American performer with an income of $400,000. Next were W. C. Fields ($155,000), Marlene Dietrich ($145,000), and Charlie Chaplin ($143,000). / Im Jahre 1934 war Mae West mit einem Einkommen von 400.000 Dollar die Spitzenverdienerin unter den Schauspielern in Amerika, gefolgt von W. C. Fields (155.000 Dollar), der Deutschen Marlene Dietrich (145.000 Dollar) und dem Briten Charlie Chaplin (143.000 Dollar). / En 1934, Mae West est l'actrice la mieux payée avec un revenu de 400 000 dollars par an. Suivent W. C. Fields (155 000 dollars), Marlene Dietrich (145 000 dollars) et Charlie Chaplin (143 000 dollars).

ON THE SET OF 'BELLE OF THE NINETIES'
(1934)
A book based on the film 'She Done Him Wrong' in the
hands of a fan. / Ein Fan hält ein Buch in der Hand,
das auf dem Film *Sie tat ihm unrecht* basiert. / Un
admirateur lui présente le livre tiré du film *Lady Lou*.

PAGES 86/87
ADVERT (1934)
Such is the speed of development at Paramount that
the Mae West films mentioned in the campaign book
sent to exhibitors were never made. / Bei Paramount
entwickelten sich die Dinge so rasant, dass die hier in
einer Werbebroschüre für Kinobesitzer erwähnten
West-Filme niemals gedreht wurden. / La roue tourne à
une vitesse folle à la Paramount : décrits dans le
catalogue publicitaire envoyé aux distributeurs, ces
films ne seront jamais tournés.

ON THE SET OF 'BELLE OF THE NINETIES'
(1934)
Veteran comedy director Leo McCarey directs a cut
scene from the film. / Leo McCarey, ein alter Hase
unter den Lustspielregisseuren, führt hier bei einer
Szene Regie, die in der endgültigen Fassung des Films
keine Verwendung fand. / Réalisateur de nombreuses
comédies, Leo McCarey dirige une scène qui sera
coupée au montage.

"Gentlemen's Choice"

A Girl Men Can't Forget. Every showman will agree that Mae West deserves first place in any book written for the box-office of this or any country. *"Gentlemen's Choice."* "Gentlemen's Choice" as a vehicle for Mae West, fits every curve of her fascinating personality and a few more not yet displayed. With this assortment of curves, blinding speed and a nice change of pace, MAE will have every film fan fanning for her, not once but again and again.

"The Queen of Sheba"

With such a title, this picture gives promise of being the greatest WESTern ever made. All about what happens when the Queen of Sheba meets King Solomon, in all his glory. *A King Can Do No Wrong?* They say that a King can do no wrong, and undoubtedly they are right, for very few Kings have had opportunities to go West . . . but don't get the idea that there is anything *wrong* with this picture . . . The Queen takes the King, that's all, and everybody's happy, Queen, King, box-office, and customers.

● Grateful exhibitors place wreath on statue of Horace Greeley, who first said, "Go WEST, young man, go WEST!"

Everybody's
goin' to Town
toda
MAE WEST
in
"GOIN' TO TOWN"
NOW PLAYING
AT THE NATION'S THEATRES
MAE WEST
in "GOIN' TO TOWN"
PARAMOUNT
Paramount Pictures

STILL FROM 'GOIN' TO TOWN' (1935)
Even though tempered by the Production Code Office, West still manages to decorate her sets with muscular males, including nude ones, at least in marble. / Obwohl der Film von der Zensur zurechtgestutzt wurde, gelang es West, ihre Kulissen mit muskulösen Mannsbildern zu schmücken, sogar mit unbekleideten – zumindest in Marmor. / Bien que refrénée par le Production Code Office, Mae West ne renonce pas aux beaux mâles, vêtus ou dénudés dans ses scènes, fussent-ils en marbre.

ADVERT FOR 'GOIN' TO TOWN' (1935)
Mae West plays Cleo Borden, a dance hall girl who inherits money, and uses it to improve her social position so that she can marry the love of her life, Carrington. / Mae West spielt Cleo Borden, eine Clubtänzerin, die mit einer Erbschaft ihre gesellschaftliche Stellung verbessert, damit sie Carrington, die Liebe ihres Lebens, heiraten kann. / Mae West incarne Cleo Borden, une danseuse de variétés qui fait un héritage et s'en sert pour gravir l'échelle sociale dans l'espoir d'épouser son grand amour, Carrington.

STILL FROM 'GOIN' TO TOWN' (1935)
Edward Carrington (Paul Cavanagh, left) is a cultured
Englishman who initially disdains Cleo's rough
manners. / Edward Carrington (Paul Cavanagh, links) ist
ein kultivierter Engländer, der Cleo anfangs aufgrund
ihrer ungehobelten Manieren verachtet. / Edward
Carrington (Paul Cavanagh, à gauche) est un gentleman
anglais, d'abord repoussé par la vulgarité de Cleo.

PORTRAIT FOR 'GOIN' TO TOWN' (1935)
The film was the beginning of West's bitter battles with
Paramount as she bridled at the restrictions put on her
by the studio. / Der Film war der Anfang der bitteren
Auseinandersetzungen zwischen West und Paramount,
weil sie die Auflagen des Studios nicht hinnehmen
wollte. / Le film marque le début d'une âpre lutte avec
la Paramount, quand Mae West se rebiffe contre les
restrictions que lui imposent les studios.

STILL FROM 'GOIN' TO TOWN' (1935)
Gigolo Ivan (Ivan Lebedeff) is in cahoots with the snooty Mrs. Brittony (Marjorie Gateson) to bring down social climber Cleo. / Gigolo Ivan (Ivan Lebedeff) tut sich mit der hochnäsigen Mrs. Brittony (Marjorie Gateson) zusammen, um Emporkömmling Cleo wieder zu Fall zu bringen. / Le gigolo Ivan (Ivan Lebedeff) est de mèche avec l'arrogante Mrs. Brittony (Marjorie Gateson) pour faire trébucher Cleo dans son ascension sociale.

ON THE SET OF 'GOIN' TO TOWN' (1935)
Director Alexander Hall, cinematographer Karl Struss (at back with glasses) and crew set up a scene in a restaurant. / Regisseur Alexander Hall, Chefkameramann Karl Struss (hinten, mit Brille) und der Stab bereiten eine Restaurantszene vor. / Tournage d'une scène dans un restaurant : entouré de l'équipe, le réalisateur Alexander Hall et le directeur de la photographie Karl Struss (à droite, avec des lunettes).

PAGES 94/95
ON THE SET OF 'GOIN' TO TOWN' (1935)
Cleo is in Buenos Aires to race her horse Cactus, ridden by jockey Taho (Tito Coral). / Cleo ist in Buenos Aires, um ihr Pferd Cactus, geritten von Jockey Taho (Tito Coral), beim Rennen antreten zu lassen. / Cleo est à Buenos Aires pour voir courir son cheval Cactus, monté par le jockey Taho (Tito Coral).

ON THE SET OF 'GOIN' TO TOWN' (1935)
In her Delilah costume, West accepts the admiration of
Lebedeff (left), Latin singer Tito Guízar (center) and
brawny Tito Coral (right). / In ihrem Delilah-Kostüm
nimmt Cleo (Mae West) die Huldigungen von Lebedeff
(links), dem Latinosänger Tito Guízar (Mitte) und dem
muskulösen Tito Coral (rechts) entgegen. / Superbe
dans son costume de Dalila, Mae sourit aux hommages
de Lebedeff (à gauche), du chanteur latino Tito Guízar
(au centre) et du musculeux Tito Coral (à droite).

STILL FROM 'GOIN' TO TOWN' (1935)
A spoof of the opera 'Samson and Delilah.' West: "I have
a lot of respect for that dame [Delilah] — there's one
lady barber that made good." / Eine Parodie der Oper
Samson and Delilah. West: „Ich hege eine Menge
Respekt für diese Dame [Delilah] — endlich ein
weiblicher Barbier, der es zu etwas gebracht hat." /
Une parodie de l'opéra *Samson et Dalila*: « Je tire mon
chapeau à cette nana [Dalila] — voilà une coiffeuse qui
a réussi. »

"It ain't no sin if you crack a few laws now and then, just so long as you don't break any."
Mae West

„Es ist keine Sünde, hin und wieder ein paar Gesetze anzuknacksen, solange man keine bricht."
Mae West

« Il n'y a pas de mal à flirter avec quelques lois de temps à autre, du moment qu'on ne les viole pas. »
Mae West

STILL FROM 'GOIN' TO TOWN' (1935)
As with most of her films, the plot complications were torturous, but it all came down to men seeking the affection of West. This film combines murder mystery, western, musical, and social comedy. / Wie die meisten ihrer Filme waren die Verwicklungen der Handlung qualvoll, aber am Ende ging es doch nur darum, dass Männer um Wests Zuneigung buhlten. Dieser Film ist eine Mischung aus Krimi, Western, Musical und Komödie. / Comme dans presque tous ses films, l'intrigue foisonne d'événements tortueux, mais se résume aux espoirs d'hommes en mal d'amour pour l'héroïne Mae West. Ce film associe meurtre mystérieux, western, music-hall et comédie dramatique.

PAGES 100/101
PAGES FROM 'PHOTOPLAY' (AUGUST, 1935)
Mae West talks about the scandal over her hidden marriage to Frank Wallace. / Mae West spricht über den Skandal ihrer heimlichen Ehe mit Frank Wallace. / Mae West évoque le scandale qu'a provoqué son mariage secret avec Frank Wallace.

MAE WEST TALKS

"I'm a single gal with a single track mind, and it doesn't run to matrimony," Mae says, emphatically

Mae West is not only an ardent fight fan (seen here at a bout), but a scrapper in her own right, as eight men who phoned and called her "wife" know to their own sorrow

"Every time the postman rings," says Mae, "I get a dozen proposals. I ought to sue 'husbands' for alienation of propositions." She's with Paul Cavanagh, "Goin' to Town"

"MARRIAGE," said Mae West, "is wonderful!"

"Of course," she added, "I'm just guessing, but it must be wonderful. Already I've got for a husband a dozen guys I've never met. Peggy Hopkins Joyce can't tie that."

Hollywood's Number One bachelor girl, grass widow or spouse (you name it) flashed her famous upper row of ivory and then curtained it quickly with serious lips. Her arched brows lowered.

"Look here," she said, "you say you want to know the truth about my 'marriage.' Well, if you want to know the truth, the whole truth and nothing but the truth, I'm beginning to get just a little burned up about this whole marriage business. It was funny for a while—even to me. Then I got a little annoyed. Now I'm getting just plain sore. I didn't mind it so much when it was just one marriage—but now it's practically bigamy!"

We were talking, of course, about the completely crazy-quilt pattern of mixed dates, double identities, confusing coincidences and controversial claims which have made the marital (or unmarital) status of La Belle West on a puzzling par with the eternal hen-egg-egg-hen dispute. Did she or didn't she? Is she or isn't she? Newspapers have even printed editorials congratulating Mae on pushing Hitler's jingoistic jitters and the Veterans' Bonus off the front page.

It was the first time Mae had unbosomed herself on the subject which she had just confessed, was giving her fits. Up until now she had contented herself with a rapid fire volley of telephonic "no's" to all questions, ranging from the laughing, amused "No" to the dangerous, now-you-lay-off-of-me "*NO!*"

"There's a saying," she reminded, "that when a woman says 'maybe' she means 'yes' and when she says 'no' she means 'maybe.' But not me. When I said 'no'—I didn't mean maybe!"

Just picture a penthouse—or anyway an apartment—'way up in the sky. All in white and gold and satin and silk. With a couple of polar bear skins spread out on the floor to lend their cooling effect to the heated lady of the house in a mood to slam the door on the Fuller brush man's foot. And all because a scattered crop of Mae Wests and Frank Wallaces had apparently put the Marrying Mdivanis to shame—and put all the answers up to Mae.

"Since the first of the year," Mae revealed, "eight different guys have called me up to tell me I married 'em. In Oshkosh or Oscaloosa, in Tulsa or Toledo. Now it's Milwaukee and points East. They've been traveling men, singing waiters dance men, reporters—but not a single millionaire—darn it!

"Which makes it bigamy—and big o'me, too, if you'll stand for a punk pun. The point is," pointed Mae, "I like a laugh, like anyone else. I've got an elastic sense of humor—but if you stretch it too far, it snaps. A gag is a gag—and if this one gave the guy a chance for a job, then it's all right, with me. But the gag has gone too far."

The determined jaw of Battling Jack West's daughter settled back into place. She smiled.

"It's all right to have a man around the house," she explained, "but when you wake up every morning to find a new husband with your grapefruit—say, I'm beginning to feel like the Dionne quintuplets. When you come up to see me now you have to look cross-eyed—or use mirrors."

"Getting down to one particular lord and master," I said "what about this Frank Wallace in New York?"

Mae dropped a stitch with her eyebrows. "Well—*what* about him?" she repeated. "I'm like Will Rogers—all I know is what I read in the papers, and I've quit reading about Wallace. I never went much for the comics, anyway."

"He says you married him in Milwaukee."

ABOUT HER "MARRIAGE"

To

KIRTLEY BASKETTE

"It was funny for a while—even to me," says Mae. "It wasn't so bad when it was just one marriage, but now it's practically bigamy!"

Frank Wallace of New York might have paraphrased the title of one of Mae's pictures, "She Done Him Wrong." He claims that Mae's denial has made him suffer

Genial Jim Timony, Mae's manager, has not escaped the "husband" touch. They labeled him such last year

"The only thing I know about Milwaukee," said Mae, "is that they make beer there. It's pretty good beer—but it never was good enough to make me get married and then forget about it."

"Then," I rallied, "he says you played Omaha."

"Wrong again," said Mae, "I picked Nellie Flag. Us girls have got to stick together," she explained. "I wish I had played Omaha," she sighed wistfully, "on the nose."

"Pardon me," I said, "but I mean the town."

Mae's "Belle of the Nineties" (with Roger Pryor) could apply to the number of males who are yelping that she deserted them

"Oh," said Mae, "I thought you meant the horse. Well, either way, it's a horse on me. I never played either one."

"This Wallace quotes certain figures," I began.

"I've heard some favorable quotes on mine," interrupted Mae.

"Let's take a look at his figures—" I began again.

"You wouldn't be interested in taking a look at mine, would you?" queried Mae. "I think it speaks for itself. What do you think?"

39

ON THE SET OF 'KLONDIKE ANNIE' (1936)
Although the press was keen to promote a rivalry
between Paramount stars Marlene Dietrich and Mae
West, the truth was that they got along fine. / Obwohl
die Presse gerne über eine Rivalität zwischen den
Paramount-Stars Marlene Dietrich und Mae West
berichtet hätte, kamen die beiden in Wahrheit gut
miteinander aus. / Marlene Dietrich et Mae West
entretenaient une relation amicale, en dépit des
allégations de la presse sur une prétendue rivalité
entre les deux stars de la Paramount.

PAGES 103–106
ADVERT FOR 'KLONDIKE ANNIE' (1936)
This innovative advert was used to sell the film to
exhibitors. / Diese innovative Anzeige diente dazu, den
Kinobesitzern den Film schmackhaft zu machen. /
Cette publicité originale servit à vendre le film aux
distributeurs.

I

Annie was a lady,
    she was 'Frisco's boast...
An' she ruled like a queen
    on the ole Barb'ry Coast.
'Til a knife-luggin' Chink
    asked Annie for a date...
So Annie up and give the town
    the Golden Gate...

Annie doesn't live here anymore

II

She grabbed her a boat
    an' she crossed the foam
To that frost-bitten,
    gal-forsaken place called Nome...
It sure didn't take her long
    to break the ice...
An' to get the boys a yellin'
    "Are we men or mice?"
She tossed 'em a smile
    an' she sang 'em a ditty
An' them sourdoughs they give her
    the skiis of the city...

"Boys, you sleigh me"

III

Te ole bennie
he got hit so hard . . .
e asked her to be
his lifetime pard . . .
a' some say as how Annie
she give 'im the wink
hen who comes in
but that 'Frisco Chink

The big bold miner tries to stake a claim to Annie's heart of gold

IV

The slant-eyed villain
he was ready to nail 'er.
But in blows a roarin',
brass-jawed sailor.
He deals that Chink
a couple o' rights
And the Chink begins
to see Northern Lights . . .

"Can't you boys learn to play?"

V

An' Annie starts a cooin'
like a turtledove
"You ferocious monster,"
says she, "I'm in love.
You're no erl painting,
You're a tough two-fister . . .
But you can take Annie
to the preacher, mister."

"You're no erl painting, but . . ."

Another good turn, please! . . .

Step up Mr. Exhibitor

And Stake Your Claim to a Real Box Office Bonanza

MAE WEST vs. **VICTOR McLAGLEN**

Spell of the Yukon   The Roaring Call of the Wild

in a swinging, singing sockeroo of a romance

"KLONDIKE ANNIE"

MAE WEST in **"KLONDIKE ANNIE"**

with **VICTOR McLAGLEN**

STILL FROM 'KLONDIKE ANNIE' (1936)
Chan Lo (Harold Huber) owns a swish nightclub and he owns Rose Carlton (Mae West) as well, keeping her caged like an exotic bird. / Chan Lo (Harold Huber) besitzt einen noblen Nachtclub und auch Rose Carlton (Mae West), die er wie einen exotischen Vogel im Käfig gefangen hält. / Chan Lo (Harold Huber) possède un night-club et une femme, Rose Carlton (Mae West), qu'il tient enfermée dans une cage dorée, comme un oiseau exotique.

ADVERT FOR 'KLONDIKE ANNIE' (1936)

STILL FROM 'KLONDIKE ANNIE' (1936)
Rose plans to escape her gilded cage and travel to the Yukon with her maid Fah Wong (Soo Yong). / Rose plant, mit ihrem Dienstmädchen Fah Wong (Soo Yong) zum Yukon aufzubrechen. / Rose prévoit de s'enfuir de sa cage dorée et de partir pour le Yukon avec sa bonne Fah Wong (Soo Yong).

PAGES 110/111
STILL FROM 'KLONDIKE ANNIE' (1936)
This scene, and many others, were cut from the film, which had to be restructured and recut many times before it was deemed suitable for release. / Diese Szene fiel, wie viele andere, der Schere zum Opfer. / Une des nombreuses scènes coupées du film, restructuré et monté plusieurs fois avant d'obtenir l'autorisation de sortie en salle.

STILL FROM 'KLONDIKE ANNIE' (1936)
Here Rose sings, "I'm an occidental woman – in an oriental mood for love." / Hier singt Rose: „I'm an occidental woman – in an oriental mood for love." („Ich bin eine Frau aus dem Abendland – in morgenländischer Liebeslaune.") / Rose chante « Je suis une femme occidentale – mais mon désir amoureux est oriental. »

STILL FROM 'KLONDIKE ANNIE' (1936)
Rose escapes on a boat, where she cares for the angelic born-again Sister Annie Alden (Helen Jerome Eddy), the woman who "saves" Rose (West). Maybe. / Rose flüchtet auf einem Schiff, wo sie sich der engels-gleichen, wiedergeborenen Schwester Annie Alden (Helen Jerome Eddy) annimmt, der Frau, die Rose (West) „rettet" — vielleicht. / Rose (Mae West) s'enfuit sur un bateau, où elle prend soin de sœur Annie Alden (Helen Jerome Eddy), un cœur pur et croyant qui « sauvera » Rose (West) — peut-être.

ON THE SET OF 'KLONDIKE ANNIE' (1936)
This bodyguard double may seem amusing, but West received death threats and promises to throw acid in her face if she testified in court about the theft of her jewelry. / Diese Doppelgängerin mag amüsant wirken, aber West erhielt Todesdrohungen und Androhungen, man werde ihr Gesicht mit Säure verätzen, wenn sie vor Gericht zum Diebstahl ihres Schmucks aussage. / La vue de ce garde du corps transformé en double de Mae prête à rire, mais l'actrice a reçu des menaces de mort et de vitriolage au cas où elle témoignerait au tribunal sur le vol de ses bijoux.

STILL FROM 'KLONDIKE ANNIE' (1936)
When Sister Annie Alden dies, Rose takes over her
identity and sincerely tries to reform the people of the
Klondike. Only Big Tess (Lucile Gleason) knows the
truth. / Als Schwester Annie Alden stirbt, nimmt Rose
ihre Identität an und versucht ernsthaft, die Menschen
am Klondike zu bekehren. Nur Big Tess (Lucile Gleason)
kennt die Wahrheit. / Quand sœur Annie Alden meurt,
Rose usurpe son identité et entreprend d'aider les gens
du Klondike. Big Tess (Lucile Gleason) est la seule à
connaître la vérité.

STILL FROM 'KLONDIKE ANNIE' (1936)
Rose falls for a wholesome policeman willing to give up everything for her. / Rose verliebt sich in einen gutmütigen Polizisten, der bereit ist, ihretwillen alles aufzugeben. / Rose s'éprend d'un brave policier, prêt à renoncer à tout pour elle.

"If I asked for a cup of coffee, someone would search for the double meaning."
Mae West

„Wenn ich eine Tasse Kaffee bestellt habe, dann hat man immer gleich nach einer Zweideutigkeit in diesem Satz gesucht."
Mae West

« Je n'ai qu'à demander une tasse de café, et quelqu'un y cherchera un sous-entendu. »
Mae West

STILL FROM 'KLONDIKE ANNIE' (1936)
Rose gives up her policeman so that he will not ruin his reputation, and she lives with Bull Brackett (Victor McLaglen). William Randolph Hearst said the film was indecent, and banned Mae West from being mentioned in his 28 newspapers. Ironically, the film had been so butchered and censored that reviewers complained about the paucity of quips! / Rose verzichtet auf ihren Polizisten, um dessen guten Ruf nicht zu ruinieren, und sie lebt mit Bull Brackett (Victor McLaglen) zusammen. William Randolph Hearst nannte den Film unanständig und verbot seinen Redakteuren, Mae West in irgendeiner seiner 28 Zeitungen zu erwähnen. / Rose quitte son policier dont elle risque de ruiner la réputation et se met en ménage avec Bull Brackett (Victor McLaglen). Outré par le film qu'il qualifie d'indécent, William Randolph Hearst interdit le nom de Mae West dans ses 28 journaux.

ON THE SET OF 'KLONDIKE ANNIE' (1936)
Mae West with costume designer Travis Banton. / Mae West mit Kostümbildner Travis Banton. / Mae West et Travis Banton qui a dessiné ses costumes.

**STILL FROM 'WHO KILLED COCK ROBIN?'
(1935)**
In 1935, when this cartoon caricature appeared, Mae
West was the top-salaried female in America with
$480,000. Only one person earned more: William
Randolph Hearst. / Im Jahre 1935, als diese Karikatur
erschien, war Mae West mit einem Jahreseinkommen
von 480.000 Dollar die höchstbezahlte Frau der USA,
und es gab nur einen Amerikaner, der mehr verdiente:
William Randolph Hearst. / En 1935, quand paraît ce
dessin satirique, Mae West est la femme la mieux payée
des États-Unis (480 000 dollars). En fait, seul un
homme gagne plus qu'elle : William Randolph Hearst.

PAGES 119–122
ADVERT FOR 'GO WEST YOUNG MAN' (1936)
To distance themselves from controversy, Paramount let
Mae West work with independent producer Emanuel
Cohen and only distributed this film and her next one.
Free from close studio supervision, West wrote a clever
screwball comedy, with a lot of sexual energy. / Um sich
von den Kontroversen zu distanzieren, ließ Paramount
Mae West mit dem unabhängigen Produzenten
Emanuel Cohen zusammenarbeiten. Von der Aufsicht
des Studios befreit schrieb West eine clevere, erotisch
geladene Screwball-Comedy. / La Paramount se
distancie des controverses en permettant à Mae West
de travailler avec le producteur indépendant Emanuel
Cohen. Libérée des contrôles du studio, Mae en profite
pour écrire une comédie farfelue, pleine de finesse et
de sex-appeal.

THIS IS THE BARN THAT GAINED RENOWN
BY HOLDING MAE'S CAR WHEN THE JALOPPY BROKE DOWN

THIS IS THE FARM WHERE SHAPELY MAE,
AS A MOVIE QUEEN DROPPED IN TO STAY

THIS IS THE APPLE THAT MAE WEST PLUCKED
FOR RANDOLPH SCOTT-WHO PROMPTLY DUCKED

THIS IS THE HEN THAT PERCHED ON THE WHEEL
OF MAE'S IMPORTED AUTOMOBILE

THIS IS THE CORN THAT GREW ON THE FARM
WHERE SCOTT RESISTED MAE WEST'S CHARM

THIS IS MAE'S PRESS AGENT, A CITY SLICKER,
WHO TOOK A BEATING WHEN HE TRIED TO TRICK HER

THIS IS THE LAD WHOSE SUNBURNED ARMS
GAVE MAE WEST A TASTE FOR FARMS

HERE IS THE ROOSTER THAT REFUSED TO CROW
UNTIL MAE TAUGHT HIM HOW TO HI-DE-HO

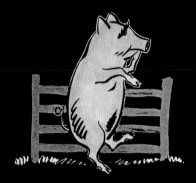

THIS IS THE PIG THAT MOPED ALL DAY
BECAUSE IT COULDN'T SWING LIKE MAE

THIS IS THE CONGRESSMAN SMART AS A WHIP
WHOM MAE SUCCEEDED IN GIVING THE SLIP

MAE WEST in
"Go West Young Man"
with
WARREN WILLIAM · RANDOLPH SCOTT
ALICE BRADY, Elizabeth Patterson, Lyle Talbot,
Isabel Jewell, Margaret Perry · Directed by
HENRY HATHAWAY · Dialogue by Mae West
An EMANUEL COHEN Production · A Paramount Picture

MAE WEST in **"Go West Young Man"**

with WARREN WILLIAM, RANDOLPH SCOTT, ALICE BRADY, Elizabeth Patterson, Lyle Talbot, Isabel Jewell,
Margaret Perry · Directed by HENRY HATHAWAY · Dialogue by Mae West · An EMANUEL COHEN Production · A Paramount Picture

STILL FROM 'GO WEST YOUNG MAN' (1936)
Mavis Arden (Mae West), a besieged movie star, trifles with handsome inventor Randolph Scott. / Mavis Arden (Mae West), ein belagerter Filmstar, tändelt mit dem gutaussehenden Erfinder Randolph Scott. / Mavis Arden (Mae West), movie star harcelée par ses admirateurs, s'amuse avec le bel inventeur, Randolph Scott.

PAGES 124/125
ON THE SET OF 'GO WEST YOUNG MAN' (1936)
Director Henry Hathaway shoots on a ranch in Corona, California. / Regisseur Henry Hathaway dreht auf einer Ranch in Corona in Kalifornien. / Tournage dans un ranch de Corona, en Californie, sous la direction de Henry Hathaway.

ADVERT FOR 'GO WEST YOUNG MAN' (1936)

STILL FROM 'GO WEST YOUNG MAN' (1936)
West comically explores the vagaries of being a star. /
Auf komische Art beschäftigt sich West mit den Launen
des Star-Seins. / Comique, Mae West explore les aléas
du statut de star.

"Save a boyfriend for a rainy day — and another,
in case it doesn't rain."
Mae West

„Heb dir immer einen guten Freund auf, falls es dir
mal schlecht geht — und einen anderen, falls nicht."
Mae West

« Gardez un amant de côté pour les jours où vous
n'allez pas bien — et un autre ... si jamais ce n'est
pas le cas. »
Mae West

STILL FROM 'GO WEST YOUNG MAN' (1936)
Warren William plays her manipulative press agent. Mae
West: "His mother should have thrown him away ... and
kept the stork." / Warren William spielt ihren manipula-
tiven Presseagenten. Mae West: „Seine Mutter hätte
ihn wegwerfen und den Storch behalten sollen." /
Warren William incarne son attaché de presse
manipulateur. Mae West : « Sa mère aurait dû le jeter ...
et garder la cigogne. »

STILL FROM 'GO WEST YOUNG MAN' (1936)
Mavis turns up the heat to 'get her man': Randolph
Scott. / Mavis dreht auf, um ihren Mann
„herumzukriegen": Randolph Scott. / Mavis a jeté son
dévolu sur Randolph Scott et joue le grand jeu pour le
séduire.

STILL FROM 'GO WEST YOUNG MAN' (1936)
Mae West: "So many men ... so little time." / Mae West:
„So viele Männer ... und so wenig Zeit." / Mae West:
« Tant d'hommes ... et si peu de temps. »

PAGES 130/131
STILL FROM 'GO WEST YOUNG MAN' (1936)
Mavis wins in the end, putting her conniving press
agent where he belongs: on the floor at her feet. /
Am Ende gewinnt Mavis und zeigt ihrem intriganten
Presseagenten, wo er hingehört: auf den Boden zu ihren
Füßen. / Mavis a fini par gagner. Elle a remis l'attaché de
presse roublard à sa place : couché à ses pieds.

**PORTRAIT FOR 'EVERY DAY'S A HOLIDAY'
(1937)**
West returns to the "gay nineties" and to costumes she
and her figure favored, designed by Elsa Schiaparelli. /
West kehrt wieder in die „fröhlichen neunziger Jahre"
des 19. Jahrhunderts zurück und zu Kostümen, die zu ihr
und ihrer Figur passten und von Elsa Schiaparelli
entworfen worden waren. / Mae revient aux années de
la Belle Époque et aux costumes si seyants pour ses
formes généreuses, réalisés par Elsa Schiaparelli.

**ON THE SET OF 'EVERY DAY'S A HOLIDAY'
(1937)**
A. Edward Sutherland (left) directs in the studio snow
of New York, circa turn of the twentieth century. /
A. Edward Sutherland (links) führt im Studioschnee
eines New Yorks der Jahrhundertwende Regie. /
Le réalisateur A. Edward Sutherland (à gauche) et Mae
dans un décor de neige en studio à New York, une
scène à l'aube du XXᵉ siècle.

STILL FROM 'EVERY DAY'S A HOLIDAY' (1937)
Cross-dressing was a motif that appeared in various
forms throughout West's theatrical and movie
productions. She was always a favorite of the gay
community. Here Charles Butterworth goes drag. /
Hier ist Charles Butterworth in Frauenkleidern zu
sehen. Der Transvestismus war ein Motiv, das sich in
unterschiedlicher Form durch Wests Theater- und
Filmproduktionen zog, und sie war in Schwulenkreisen
stets beliebt. / Le travestissement sous toutes ses
formes est un thème fréquent dans les productions
cinématographiques et théâtrales de Mae West.
L'actrice a toujours été une icône de la communauté
gay. Ici, Charles Butterworth joue un travesti.

*"A man can be short and dumpy and getting bald
but if he has fire, women will like him."*
Mae West

*„Ein Mann kann klein und dick sein und die Haare
verlieren, aber wenn Feuer in ihm steckt, dann
werden ihn die Frauen lieben."*
Mae West

STILL FROM 'EVERY DAY'S A HOLIDAY' (1937)
Walter Catlett as Nifty Bailey, one of the many
wonderful character actors who populated this film. /
Walter Catlett als Nifty Bailey, einer der vielen
wunderbaren Charakterdarsteller, die diesen Film
bevölkerten. / Un des superbes seconds rôles qui
peuplent ce film, Walter Catlett incarne Nifty Bailey.

PAGES 136/137
STILL FROM 'EVERY DAY'S A HOLIDAY' (1937)
West lost weight for the part and featured her new
figure, still voluptuous but more streamlined. / West
nahm für diese Rolle ab und zeigte ihre neue Figur —
immer noch üppig, aber etwas stromlinienförmiger. /
Mae West a minci pour ce rôle ; elle exhibe sa nouvelle
silhouette, toujours sensuelle, mais aux lignes plus
aérodynamiques.

« Qu'un homme soit petit, ventripotent et chauve,
s'il a le feu en lui, les femmes l'aimeront. »
Mae West

STILL FROM 'EVERY DAY'S A HOLIDAY' (1937)
Peaches O'Day, who is happy to sell the Brooklyn Bridge
to suckers, and her personal human trio of "three
monkeys." / Peaches O'Day, glücklich, Trotteln die
Brooklyn Bridge zu verkaufen, und ihr persönliches
„Affentrio". / Peaches O'Day se réjouit de vendre le
pont de Brooklyn à des pigeons devant son trio
personnel, les « trois singes ».

STILL FROM 'EVERY DAY'S A HOLIDAY' (1937)
Lloyd Nolan as the corrupt inspector confronting the
morally ambiguous Peaches, here disguised as
Mademoiselle Fifi. / Lloyd Nolan spielt den korrupten
Inspektor, der die moralisch zweideutige Peaches – hier
verkleidet als Mademoiselle Fifi – zur Rede stellt. /
Lloyd Nolan, inspecteur corrompu, demande des
comptes à Peaches. La belle à la moralité ambiguë s'est
déguisée en Mademoiselle Fifi.

"I wrote the story myself. It's about a girl who lost her reputation and never missed it."
Mae West

"Ich habe die Geschichte selbst geschrieben. Es geht um ein Mädchen, das seinen guten Ruf verloren und nie vermisst hat."
Mae West

« J'ai écrit moi-même l'histoire. Il s'agit d'une fille qui a perdu sa réputation, et n'a jamais tenté de la retrouver. »
Mae West

PORTRAIT FOR 'EVERY DAY'S A HOLIDAY' (1937)
Mademoiselle Fifi is a delight to audiences on screen and off. Mae West: "When women go wrong, men go right after them." / Mademoiselle Fifi bereitet dem Publikum auf der Leinwand und außerhalb des Kinos Vergnügen. Mae West: „Wo Mädchen auf die schiefe Bahn geraten, laufen die Männer geradewegs hinterher." / Mademoiselle Fifi est adorée du public à l'écran et dans la vie. Mae West: « Quand une fille prend le mauvais chemin, les hommes courent tout droit ... derrière elle. »

MAE WEST, CHARLIE MCCARTHY & EDGAR BERGEN (1937)
Even "men of wood" are not immune to West's sexual allure — Charlie McCarthy with hand on breast as Edgar Bergen tries to keep his puppet in rein. Mae did a sketch on their radio show which got her banned by NBC. / Selbst „Männer aus Holz" können sich Wests Sex-Appeal kaum entziehen — hier legt ihr Charlie McCarthy die Hand auf die Brust, während Bauch-redner Edgar Bergen versucht, seine Puppe im Zaum zu halten. In der Rundfunksendung der beiden spielte Mae einen Sketch, für den sie von NBC Senderverbot erhielt. / Même les « hommes en bois » ne sont pas immunisés contre le sex-appeal de Mae West : main sur le cœur, Charlie McCarthy joue Edgar Bergen qui essaie de sauver la vertu de sa marionnette. Après un sketch dans son émission radiophonique, Mae West sera bannie de NBC.

PAGES 143–146
ADVERT FOR 'MY LITTLE CHICKADEE' (1940)
After being labelled 'box office poison' by exhibitors in 1937, it took 3 years for Mae West to get back in the saddle, and she had to share it with W. C. Fields. / Nachdem die Kinobesitzer sie 1937 als „Kassengift" gebrandmarkt hatten, brauchte Mae West drei Jahre, um wieder Fuß zu fassen, und sie musste sich dann das Rampenlicht mit W. C. Fields teilen. / En 1937, qualifiée de « poison du box-office » par les distributeurs, Mae West attendra trois ans pour se remettre en selle, et devra la partager avec W. C. Fields.

MAE WEST

YIPPEE!

IN UNIVERSAL'S ROOTIN', HOLDOVER TOOTIN', SAGA-DAGA OF THE WEST!

"MY LITTLE CHICKADEE"

With Joseph Calleia · Dick Foran · Donald Meek · Fuzzy Knight
Margaret Hamilton · Ruth Donnelly

DIRECTED BY EDWARD CLINE

PRODUCED BY LESTER COWAN

YEE-OW! RIDE THAT SHOWMANSHIP!

W.C. FIELDS!

YAHOO!

OUT WEST—where Mae has room for her "hip-notic" ways!

WAY OUT WEST—where the mighty Bill Fields can dodge with the best!

WAY, WAY OUT WEST—where the funniest twain in hic-history meets and shakes every tepee to its baggy foundation.

ADDLE WITH UNIVERSAL, PARDNER!

IT'S A TRAIL OF GOLDEN DATES!
Starting
FEBRUARY
9th
NATIONAL
RELEASE!
So Hop on Your Pinto, and
Reserve a Print-o... at
Your Universal Exchange,
NOW!

STILL FROM 'MY LITTLE CHICKADEE' (1940)
Flower Belle Lee (Mae West) is run out of town because she dallied with the Masked Bandit. Mrs. Gideon (Margaret Hamilton) was not the only one "sour" during the shooting of this film. / Flower Belle Lee (Mae West) wird aus der Stadt gejagt, weil sie sich mit dem „maskierten Banditen" eingelassen hat. Mrs. Gideon (Margaret Hamilton) war nicht die einzige, die bei den Dreharbeiten zu diesem Film „sauer" wurde. / Flower Belle Lee (Mae West) est chassée de la ville pour s'être acoquinée avec le Bandit masqué. Mrs. Gideon (Margaret Hamilton) n'est pas la seule à montrer sa mauvaise humeur durant le tournage de ce film.

ADVERT FOR 'MY LITTLE CHICKADEE' (1940)
Both W. C. Fields and Mae West wrote their own dialogue, as usual, and shared credit for the screenplay. / Sowohl W. C. Fields als auch Mae West schrieben, wie üblich, ihre Texte selbst und wurden als Mitautoren des Drehbuchs genannt. / Comme à leur habitude, W. C. Fields et Mae West écrivent leurs propres dialogues ; tous deux auteurs du scénario, leurs noms sont associés au générique.

STILL FROM 'MY LITTLE CHICKADEE' (1940)
Believing she was playing second fiddle to W. C. Fields,
West said: "I sorta stepped off my pedestal when I
made that movie." / In der Überzeugung, dass sie neben
W. C. Fields die zweite Geige spielte, sagte West: „Als
ich diesen Film drehte, bin ich in gewisser Weise von
meinem Sockel runtergestiegen." / Persuadée qu'elle
n'a servi que de faire-valoir à W. C. Fields, Mae West
déclare : « Ma foi, je suis tombée de mon piédestal en
tournant ce film. »

STILL FROM 'MY LITTLE CHICKADEE' (1940)
Cuthbert J. Twillie (W. C. Fields) marries Flower Belle
but finds it hard to consummate the new concatenation.
Twillie: "New is right. She hasn't been unwrapped yet." /
Cuthbert J. Twillie (W. C. Fields) heiratet Flower Belle,
aber er hat Schwierigkeiten, die neue Verbindung zu
vollziehen. Twillie: „Neu stimmt. Sie ist noch nicht
ausgepackt." / Cuthbert J. Twillie (W. C. Fields) épouse
Flower Belle, une union qui ne semble pas vraiment
l'« emballer ». Twillie : « C'est le cas de le dire : je ne l'ai
pas encore déballée. »

STILL FROM 'MY LITTLE CHICKADEE' (1940)
Twillie becomes bartender, card shark, and sheriff of
Greasewood City. Flower Belle allows the men,
including saloon owner Jeff Badger (Joseph Calleia,
left), to pay her some attention. / Twillie wird Barmann,
Kartenhai und Sheriff von Greasewood City. Flower
Belle gestattet den Männern – darunter Saloonbesitzer
Jeff Badger (Joseph Calleia, links) –, sich ihr gegenüber
aufmerksam zu zeigen. / Twillie devient barman, un
requin aux cartes et le shérif de Greasewood City.
Flower Belle accepte les hommages masculins, y
compris ceux de Jeff Badger (Joseph Calleia, à gauche),
le propriétaire du saloon.

*"He's the kind of man a woman would have to
marry to get rid of."*
Mae West

„*Er ist die Art von Mann, den eine Frau heiraten
müsste, um ihn loszuwerden.*"
Mae West

STILL FROM 'MY LITTLE CHICKADEE' (1940)
The erotic appeal of the Masked Bandit (Joseph
Calleia). Mae West: "Between two evils, I always pick
the one I never tried before." / Die erotische
Anziehungskraft des „maskierten Banditen" (Joseph
Calleia). Mae West: „Wenn ich zwischen zwei Übeln
wählen muss, suche ich mir immer das aus, das ich
vorher noch nicht ausprobiert habe." / Le Bandit
masqué (Joseph Calleia) à l'aura érotique. Mae West:
« De deux démons, je choisis toujours celui que je n'ai
pas encore essayé. »

*« C'est le type d'homme qu'il faudrait épouser ...
pour s'en débarrasser. »*
Mae West

PAGES 152/153
**ON THE SET OF 'MY LITTLE CHICKADEE'
(1940)**
With director Edward Cline filming, Flower Belle agrees
to take over classes from the ailing schoolteacher.
Flower Belle (to boys): "One and one is two, and two
and two is four, and five will get you ten if you know how
to work it." / Während Regisseur Edward F. Cline filmt,
erklärt sich Flower Belle bereit, die Klasse einer
erkrankten Lehrerin zu übernehmen. Flower Belle (zu
den Jungen): „Eins plus eins ist zwei, und zwei und zwei
macht vier, und aus fünf kannst du zehn machen, wenn
du weißt, wie man es anstellt." / Devant la caméra du
réalisateur Edward Cline, Flower Belle accepte de
remplacer l'institutrice malade. Flower Belle (aux
garçons de l'école) : « Un et un font deux, deux et deux
font quatre, et avec cinq vous en obtiendrez dix si vous
savez comment vous y prendre. »

"Is that a gun in your pocket or are you just happy to see me?"
Mae West

„Ist das ein Revolver in Ihrer Tasche, oder freuen Sie sich nur, mich zu sehen?"
Mae West

« T'as un revolver dans ta poche, ou t'es content de me voir ? »
Mae West

STILL FROM 'MY LITTLE CHICKADEE' (1940)
In this quasi-Western, West seizes the traditional male symbol of power — the gun — two of them of course. / In diesem Quasiwestern greift sich West das traditionelle männliche Machtsymbol: das Schießeisen — und natürlich gleich doppelt. / Dans ce pseudo-western, Mae West s'empare du symbole par excellence de la virilité (le revolver), deux à la fois naturellement.

ON THE SET OF 'MY LITTLE CHICKADEE' (1940)
West was a keen sports fan. Here she listens to a football game with the crew. / West war ein großer Sportfan. Hier hört sie sich mit dem Stab ein Footballspiel an. / Mae West était une fan de sport. Sur le plateau, elle écoute un match de football américain à la radio, entourée de l'équipe de tournage.

STILL FROM 'MY LITTLE CHICKADEE' (1940)
In the closing scene, Fields and West swap catchphrases. Twillie: "If you get up around the Grampian Hills — why don't you come up and see me sometime?" Flower Belle: " Ah, yeah, yeah, I'll do that, my little chickadee." / In der Schlussszene tauschen Fields und West die Sprüche aus. Twillie: „Wenn du mal in die Grampian Hills kommst, warum kommst du nicht mal rauf und schaust bei mir vorbei?" Flower Belle: „Ah, ja, ja, das werde ich tun, mein kleiner Gockel." / Réparties de Fields et West dans la scène finale. Twillie : «Si tu passes un de ces jours par les Grampian Hills, viens me rendre une petite visite. » Flower Belle : « Mais oui, mon petit poussin, bien sûr que je viendrai. »

STILL FROM 'THE HEAT'S ON' (1943)
West did not like the banal script but appeared as a
favor to friend and director Gregory Ratoff. Mae West:
"A man in the house ... is worth two in the street." /
West gefiel das banale Drehbuch nicht, aber sie nahm
die Rolle aus Gefälligkeit gegenüber ihrem Freund, dem
Regisseur Gregory Ratoff, an. Mae West: „Ein Mann im
Haus ... ist so viel wert wie zwei auf der Straße." / Bien
qu'elle trouve le scénario trop banal, Mae West
acceptera le rôle par amitié pour le réalisateur Gregory
Ratoff. Mae West: « Un homme à la maison ... en vaut
deux dans la rue. »

*"An ounce of performance is worth pounds of
promises."*
Mae West

*„Ein Gramm Leistung ist so viel wert wie Pfunde
Versprechungen."*
Mae West

*« Une once de performance vaut mieux que des
kilos de promesses. »*
Mae West

STILL FROM 'THE HEAT'S ON' (1943)
Except for a couple of lame musical numbers, and some unfunny scenes that she did not write, West had little to do. Mae West: "Ten men waiting for me at the door? Send one of them home, I'm tired." / Abgesehen von ein paar lahmen Musikeinlagen und einigen unlustigen Szenen, die nicht sie geschrieben hatte, blieb für West wenig zu tun. Mae West: „Zehn Männer warten an der Tür auf mich? Schick einen von ihnen nach Hause – ich bin müde." / Le rôle de Mae West se résume à deux ou trois numéros de variétés sans pep et quelques scènes ennuyeuses qui ne sont pas de son cru. Mae West : «Dix hommes m'attendent à la porte ? Renvoyez-en un, je suis épuisée. »

STILL FROM 'THE HEAT'S ON' (1943)
Fay Lawrence (Mae West) vamps Hubert Bainbridge (Victor Moore) as a middle-aged investor who is too excited to keep his toupee straight. / Fay Lawrence (Mae West) wickelt Hubert Bainbridge (Victor Moore) um den Finger, einen Investor mittleren Alters, dem vor lauter Aufregung das Toupet verrutscht. / Fay Lawrence (Mae West) embobine Hubert Bainbridge (Victor Moore), un actionnaire d'âge mûr, si excité qu'il en perd presque sa moumoute.

PORTRAIT FOR 'THE HEAT'S ON' (1943)
A dress worthy of an icon, by costume designer Walter Plunkett. Mae West: "Those who are easily shocked should be shocked more often." / Ein Kleid, das einer Ikone würdig ist, entworfen von Kostümbildner Walter Plunkett. Mae West: „Diejenigen, die leicht zu schockieren sind, sollten vielleicht öfter mal schockiert werden." / Un costume digne d'une icône, dessiné par le styliste Walter Plunkett. Mae West : « Ceux qui se choquent facilement devraient le faire plus souvent. »

COVER OF THEATER PROGRAM FOR 'DIAMOND LIL' (1949)

PAGES 164/165
PAGES FROM THEATER PROGRAM FOR 'DIAMOND LIL' (1949)

SIGNED PAGE OF THEATER PROGRAM FOR 'DIAMOND LIL' (1949)
Mae West: "She's the kind of girl who climbed the ladder of success wrong by wrong." / Mae West: „Sie ist die Art von Mädchen, die die Leiter des Erfolgs auf krummen Wegen erklommen hat." / Mae West : « C'est le genre de fille qui a grimpé l'échelle du succès faux pas à faux pas. »

SCENES FROM "DIAMOND LIL"

THE SAGA OF "DIAMOND LIL"

ABULOUS MAE WEST first saw the light of day in Brooklyn, U.S.A., and inasmuch as one good deed deserves another, it was this self-same Brooklyn which first saw the bright light of Mae West as "Diamond Lil." It was early Spring, 1928, when "Diamond Lil" made her stage debut at an obscure theatre in Brooklyn. Critical acclaim from drama reviewer Robert Garland brought Miss West and "Diamond Lil" to the attention of the across-the-river Broadway theatregoers and managers and in order to make it much easier on everyone concerned, Mae West packed her self-written play complete with beer, diamonds and famous slink, and crossed the famous Bridge to Manhattan where she launched her New York production at the Royale Theatre on the night of April 9, 1928. For six long months, Mae West was "Diamond Lil" and vice was versa. Her spoofing of sex, crime and the Gay Nineties actually became the foundation for her subsequent great success on stage and screen here and abroad.

In brief, the story of "Diamond Lil" takes place on the Bowery in the year of 1898. As Queen of the Bowery, "Diamond Lil" is headmistress at Gus Jordon's Saloon. Needless to say, Gus Jordon is Master. During the course of the play (while her beer-tapping boy-friend is conveniently off-stage) "Lil" indulges in some extra curricular amatory activities with a handsome, brawny Salvation Army Captain, a dashing latin lover, a menacing would-be district leader, a has-been discarded lover and assorted male admirers. Complications ensue quite naturally and these complications include white-slavery, dope-peddling, man-slaughter, double-crossing, political chicanery and love-making as practiced

in the good old days. In the end, the Salvation Army Captain turns out to be a captain of a different color—a police captain who has masqueraded as the incorruptible Salvation Army man in order to get the goods on Big Boss Gus Jordon.

The hero's sudden unmasking does not disappoint "Lil" insofar as she had already tired of the old boy-friend. As the last act curtain falls, the newly-acquired boy-friend is met more than halfway on his way up to see her, sans tambourine and thereby free to prove to "Lil" that she was right from the start when she said she always knew he "could be had."

Following its sensational New York run at the Royale, Mae West and "Diamond Lil" toured the country from coast-to-coast. One of her greatest screen triumphs, "She Done Him Wrong" was a filmization of "Diamond Lil" and last year when Miss West went to England to star in this production she scored one of the truly great successes of all time, when before royalty and commoner alike, she slinked through the play for ten long months and broke box-office records established by the leading stars of the English speaking stage. This present production is more lavish than the original, more elaborate than her European presentation. Mae West as "Diamond Lil" is as important a part of the American scene, the American way of life as is the rolling plains, the towering skyscrapers, the "hot dog" and the Atomic Bomb. She and "Diamond Lil" are as solid as the Plymouth Rock and as provocative as the Kinsey Report. There seems to be no end in sight for Mae West as "Diamond Lil" and that's a mighty good thing to know, these days!

FROM THE PLAY 'DIAMOND LIL' (1949)
Mae West: "Why don't you come on up and see me sometime ... when I've got nothin' on but the radio." / Mae West: „Warum kommst du nicht mal rauf und schaust mal vorbei ... wenn ich nichts anhabe außer dem Radio." / Mae West : « Viens donc me voir un de ces jours, quand je n'aurai rien mis ... sauf la radio. »

PORTRAIT FOR THE PLAY 'DIAMOND LIL' (1949)
Mae West successfully returned to the stage in 1944 with 'Catherine Was Great,' and then had several revivals of 'Diamond Lil' in America and touring the UK. / Mae West kehrte 1944 mit dem Stück *Catherine Was Great* erfolgreich auf die Bühne zurück, und danach gab es mehrere Wiederaufführungen von *Diamond Lil* in Amerika und auf einer Tournee durch Großbritannien. / En 1944, Mae West fait un retour glorieux sur les planches avec la pièce *Catherine Was Great* ; elle rejoue plusieurs fois *Diamond Lil* aux États-Unis et part en tournée en Grande-Bretagne.

PORTRAIT
Exercising to keep in shape for her fans. She was a
health food advocate and spiritualist. / Mit sportlichen
Übungen hielt sie sich fit für ihre Fans. Sie machte sich
für Reformkost stark und wurde zur Anhängerin des
Spiritismus. / Mae West se maintient en forme par
respect pour ses admirateurs. La star prône la
diététique et s'intéresse au spiritualisme.

MICKEY HARGITAY & MAE WEST (1954)
Mickey Hargitay was one of the many buff men in her
touring 'muscleman' show, which appealed to gay
audiences with its camp humor and visuals. Mae West:
"I go for two kinds of men. The kind with muscles, and
the kind without." / Mickey Hargitay war einer der
vielen gutgebauten Männer in der „Muskelmänner"-
Show, mit der sie auf Tournee ging und die
insbesondere bei Homosexuellen großen Anklang
fand mit ihrem tuntenhaften Humor und ihrer
entsprechenden Ausstattung. Mae West: „Ich stehe auf
zwei Sorten von Männern: die mit Muskeln und die
ohne." / Mickey Hargitay, un des culturistes de son show
de variétés qui remporte un franc succès auprès du
public gay pour son humour effronté et ses plastiques
masculines. Mae West : « J'aime deux types d'hommes,
ceux avec des muscles, et ceux sans. »

ON THE SET OF 'MYRA BRECKINRIDGE' (1970)

The diva returns to the screen in an adaptation of Gore Vidal's gender-bending Hollywood satire. Mae West plays voracious agent Leticia Van Allen. / Mit einer Verfilmung von Gore Vidals Travestiekomödie kehrt die Diva auf die Leinwand zurück. Mae West spielt die unersättliche Agentin Leticia Van Allen. / La diva retourne à l'écran dans une adaptation hollywoodienne de la satire de la transsexualité signée Gore Vidal. Mae West incarne Leticia Van Allen, un féroce agent artistique.

ON THE SET OF 'MYRA BRECKINRIDGE' (1970)

Director Michael Sarne on his knee. He told reporters that he wanted Mae West for the part because of her lifelong association with drag queen culture. Leticia Van Allen: "Well, the end of another busy day. I can't wait till I get back to bed. If that don't work I'll try to sleep." / Regisseur Michael Sarne auf Knien. Er erzählte Reportern, dass er Mae West für diese Rolle haben wollte, weil sie schon ihr ganzes Leben lang mit Transvestiten zu tun hatte. / Michael Sarne à genoux. Le réalisateur confia à des journalistes qu'il voulait Mae West pour le rôle en raison de ses liens privilégiés avec le milieu travesti.

PORTRAIT FOR 'MYRA BRECKINRIDGE' (1970)
This shot crystallizes the camp quality of the movie —
Buck Loner (John Huston), Myra (Raquel Welch), Leticia
Van Allen (Mae West), and Myron (Rex Reed). / Diese
Aufnahme bringt das Tuntenhafte des Films auf den
Punkt: Buck Loner (John Huston), Myra (Raquel Welch),
Leticia Van Allen (Mae West) und Myron (Rex Reed). /
Cette prise de vue capte la fantaisie délurée du film.
Buck Loner (John Huston), Myra (Raquel Welch), Leticia
Van Allen (Mae West) et Myron (Rex Reed).

"I used to be Snow White, but I drifted."
Mae West

*„Ich war mal ein Schneewittchen, aber ich bin
verweht worden."*
Mae West

*« J'étais une "Blanche-Neige", mais j'ai glissé sur la
mauvaise pente. »*
Mae West

**ON THE SET OF 'MYRA BRECKINRIDGE'
(1970)**
A very young, impressed, and handsome Tom Selleck as
The Stud. Stud: "A bed! I never did see a bed in an
office before." Leticia Van Allen: "Well, you see I, I do
a lot of night work sometimes." / Ein sehr junger,
gutaussehender und sichtlich beeindruckter Tom
Selleck, als der „Hengst". Er: „Ein Bett! Ich hab noch nie
zuvor ein Bett in einem Büro gesehen." Leticia Van
Allen: „Nun, ich ... ich mache sehr viel Nachtarbeit." /
Jeune, beau et intimidé, Tom Selleck interprète Stud :
« Un lit ! Je n'ai encore jamais vu un lit dans un bureau. »
Leticia Van Allen : « Eh bien, vois-tu, je ... je travaille
parfois beaucoup la nuit. »

"To err is human — but it feels divine."
Mae West

*„Irren ist menschlich — aber es fühlt sich
göttlich an."*
Mae West

*« L'erreur est humaine, mais elle a quelque chose
de divin. »*
Mae West

PORTRAIT FOR RECORD 'WAY OUT WEST' (1966)

In 1966 the ever-youthful West recorded an album of contemporary songs by the Beatles and others, often inserting her own words and catchphrases. / Im Jahre 1966 nahm die stets junggebliebene West ein Album mit zeitgenössischen Songs der Beatles und anderer Künstler auf, wobei oft ihre eigenen Worte und Pointen in die Liedtexte einflossen. / En 1966, Mae West, à la jeunesse éternelle, enregistre un album de chansons des Beatles et d'autres artistes contemporains, truffant souvent les textes de ses propres réparties.

"You only live once, but if you do it right, once is enough."
Mae West

„Man lebt nur einmal, aber wenn man's richtig macht, dann reicht das aus."
Mae West

« On ne vit qu'une fois, mais si on le fait bien, une fois suffit. »
Mae West

STILL FROM 'BACKLOT USA' (1976)
83-year-old West appeared with Henry Fonda on Dick
Cavett's tribute to classic Hollywood, and performed
two songs. / Mit 83 Jahren trat West mit Henry Fonda in
Dick Cavetts Hommage an das klassische Hollywood
auf und sang zwei Lieder. / Mae West à l'âge de 83 ans,
aux côtés de Henry Fonda lors de l'émission de Dick
Cavett en hommage à Hollywood ; elle y interprète
deux chansons.

STILL FROM 'SEXTETTE' (1978)
With Timothy Dalton. Mae West: "I only like two kinds of men, domestic and imported." / An der Seite von Timothy Dalton. Mae West: „Ich mag nur zwei Sorten Männer: einheimische und ausländische." / Aux côtés de Timothy Dalton. Mae West: « J'aime seulement deux sortes d'hommes, ceux d'ici et ceux d'ailleurs. »

PAGE 178
PORTRAIT (1928)
Mae West: "I like my clothes to be tight enough to show I'm a woman ... but loose enough to show I'm a lady." / Mae West: „Ich mag es, wenn meine Kleider so eng sind, dass man sieht, dass ich eine Frau bin, und weit genug, um zu zeigen, dass ich eine Dame bin." / Mae West: « J'aime les vêtements assez moulants pour montrer que je suis une femme ... et assez amples pour montrer que je suis une lady. »

STILL FROM 'SEXTETTE' (1978)
West returns to the screen one last time in this revival of her play. Mae West: "Marriage is a great institution, but I'm not ready for an institution." / In dieser Wiederaufführung ihres Theaterstücks kehrte West ein letztes Mal auf die Leinwand zurück. Mae West: „Die Ehe ist eine großartige ‚institution' [‚Institution'], aber ich bin noch nicht reif für die ‚institution' [engl. auch: ‚Anstalt']." / Dernière apparition de la star à l'écran dans une adaptation de sa pièce. Mae West: « Le mariage est une institution remarquable, mais je ne suis pas faite pour les institutions [jeu de mot: angl. "institution" = institution/hospice]. »

3
CHRONOLOGY

CHRONOLOGIE

CHRONOLOGIE

CHRONOLOGY

17 August 1893 Born Mary Jane West in Brooklyn, New York.

1897–1911 First appearances on stage as a child performer in vaudeville and burlesque.

1911 Joins a stock company run by Hal Clarendon. Marries vaudevillian Frank Wallace.

1912 Begins performing regularly at Hammerstein's, one of the primary vaudeville venues in New York.

1917 Semi-retires from vaudeville, disappointed with her lack of stardom, and pursues writing.

1926 Her play *Sex* debuts as does *The Drag*. *The Drag* sympathizes with the plight of gay men and transvestite performers.

1927 Sentenced for ten days in Welfare Island jail for public obscenity for her play *Sex*. Undaunted, she later opens another controversial play, *The Wicked Age*.

1928 Her play *Diamond Lil* becomes a huge Broadway success. Her gender-bending play *Pleasure Man* debuts. Begins her lifelong study of spiritualism and health foods.

1930 Publishes erotic novel *Babe Gordon*.

1931 Her play *The Constant Sinner* opens, causing more controversy for its subject of miscegenation.

1932 Makes her film debut in *Night After Night* with George Raft.

1933 Paramount takes a chance on *Diamond Lil* but changes its name to *She Done Him Wrong*. It is a major success. *I'm No Angel*, West's next film, leads to calls for stricter censorship in movies and enforcement of the largely ignored Production Code.

1934 West's script *It Ain't No Sin* is toned down and made into *Belle of the Nineties* due to

pressure from the newly invigorated Production Code office.

1935 *Goin' to Town* is the beginning of the end as Paramount attempts to reform West's sexually transgressive screen image.

1936 West is a morally reborn dance hall performer in *Klondike Annie*. With Randolph Scott in *Go West Young Man*.

1937 *Every Day's a Holiday* costs too much and does not perform at the box office. Mae West is labeled "Box-Office Poison" by exhibitors.

1940 *My Little Chickadee* with W. C. Fields.

1943 *The Heat's On* features West in little more than a walk-on.

1944 Her play *Catherine Was Great* debuts. West believed she was the reincarnation of Catherine the Great.

1948 Begins touring with *Diamond Lil* in New York and London.

1954 Begins a series of tours with a nightclub act featuring musclemen as chorus boys.

1959 Publishes her autobiography, *Goodness Had Nothing to Do With It*.

1961 Writes the play *Sextette*.

1970 West returns to the screen at age 77 and plays Leticia Van Allen in Gore Vidal's *Myra Breckinridge*.

1978 Plays Marlo Manners/Lady Barrington in film adaptation of her *Sextette*.

22 November 1980 Dies of a stroke in Hollywood.

COVER OF 'POPULAR SONGS' (AUGUST 1935)

CHRONOLOGIE

17. August 1893 Sie kommt als Mary Jane West in Brooklyn, New York, zur Welt.

1897–1911 Erster Bühnenauftritt als Kinderdarstellerin im Varieté.

1911 Sie tritt einem Schauspielerensemble um Hal Clarendon bei und heiratet den Varietékünstler Frank Wallace.

1912 Sie tritt regelmäßig im Hammerstein's auf, einer der führenden New Yorker Varietébühnen.

1917 Aus Enttäuschung über ihren mangelnden Erfolg zieht sie sich vorläufig aus dem Varieté zurück und beginnt zu schreiben.

1926 Ihre Stücke *Sex* und *The Drag* werden uraufgeführt. *The Drag* zeigt Verständnis für die Notlage homosexueller Männer und Travestiekünstler.

1927 Wegen öffentlicher Unzucht wird sie aufgrund ihres Theaterstücks *Sex* zu zehn Tagen Gefängnis auf Welfare Island verurteilt. Ohne sich einschüchtern zu lassen, bringt sie kurz darauf ein weiteres umstrittenes Stück auf die Bühne, *The Wicked Age*.

1928 Ihr Theaterstück *Diamond Lil* wird ein großer Erfolg am Broadway. Ihr Transvestitenstück *Pleasure Man* wird uraufgeführt. Sie beginnt ihre lebenslang währende Beschäftigung mit Spiritismus und Diätkost.

1930 Sie veröffentlicht den erotischen Roman *Babe Gordon*.

1931 Ihr Theaterstück *The Constant Sinner* wird uraufgeführt und führt mit seinem Thema der Rassenmischung zu weiteren Kontroversen.

1932 Sie feiert ihr Filmdebüt in *Night After Night* mit George Raft.

1933 Paramount riskiert eine Verfilmung von *Diamond Lil*, ändert den Titel aber um in *Sie tat ihm*

unrecht. Der Film wird ein Riesenerfolg. Wests nächster Film, *Ich bin kein Engel*, führt zu Forderungen nach einer strengeren Zensur und zu einer strikteren Durchsetzung der bislang ignorierten Produktionsrichtlinien.

1934 Wests Drehbuch *It Ain't No Sin* wird unter dem Druck der erstarkten Filmselbstzensur (Production Code Office) abgemildert und unter dem Titel *Belle of the Nineties* verfilmt.

1935 *Goin' to Town* ist der Anfang vom Ende für Paramounts Versuche, Wests Leinwandimage der sexuellen Tabubrecherin zu läutern.

1936 West spielt in *Klondike Annie* ein leichtes Mädchen, das auf den Pfad der Tugend zurückgefunden hat und mit Randolph Scott in *Auf in den Westen*.

1937 *Every Day's a Holiday* ist zu teuer und erzielt kein gutes Einspielergebnis. Daraufhin erklären die Kinobesitzer Mae West zum „Kassengift".

1940 *Mein kleiner Gockel* mit W. C. Fields.

1943 In *The Heat's On* spielt West kaum mehr als eine Komparsenrolle.

1944 Ihr Theaterstück *Catherine Was Great* wird uraufgeführt. West glaubte, sie sei die Reinkarnation Katharinas der Großen.

1948 Sie geht mit ihrem Stück *Diamond Lil* in New York und London auf Tournee.

1954 Sie beginnt eine Reihe von Tourneen mit einer Nachtclubnummer, in der Muskelprotze als Chorknaben auftreten.

1959 Sie veröffentlicht ihre Autobiografie *Goodness Had Nothing to Do With It*.

1961 Sie schreibt das Stück *Sextette*.

1970 West kehrt mit 77 noch einmal auf die Leinwand zurück und spielt Leticia Van Allen in Gore Vidals *Myra Breckinridge*.

1978 Sie spielt Marlo Manners/Lady Barrington in einer Verfilmung ihres Theaterstücks *Sextette*.

22. November 1980 Sie stirbt in Hollywood an einem Schlaganfall.

PORTRAIT

Mae West: "You may admire a girl's curves on the first introduction ... but the second meeting shows up new angles." / Mae West: „Wenn man eine Frau kennenlernt, dann bewundert man vielleicht ihre Kurven — aber bei der zweiten Begegnung zeigen sich dann die Ecken und Kanten." / Mae West: « Tu peux admirer les courbes d'une fille à la première rencontre ... mais à la deuxième, tu découvres de nouveaux angles. »

CHRONOLOGIE

17 août 1893 Naissance de Mary Jane West à Brooklyn, New York.

1897–1911 Premières apparitions, dès l'âge de quatre ans, sur les planches dans des vaudevilles et des comédies burlesques.

1911 Rejoint une compagnie théâtrale dirigée par Hal Clarendon. Épouse Frank Wallace, un acteur de variétés.

1912 Prestations régulières au Hammerstein's, l'un des premiers théâtres de vaudeville de New York.

1917 Quitte en partie le vaudeville, déçue par une carrière et une popularité médiocres.

1926 Création de ses pièces *Sex* et *The Drag*. *The Drag* prend fait et cause pour les homosexuels et les travestis.

1927 Sa pièce *Sex* lui vaut dix jours de prison pour obscénité publique, à la Welfare Island Jail. Sans se laisser intimider, elle monte ensuite une autre pièce osée *The Wicked Age*.

1928 Sa pièce *Diamond Lil* remporte un énorme succès à Broadway. Première de la pièce *Pleasure Man* qui joue sur le masculin/féminin. Début de son intérêt pour la spiritualité et la diététique, qui durera jusqu'à sa mort.

1930 Publie une nouvelle érotique intitulée *Babe Gordon*.

1931 Première de sa pièce *The Constant Sinner* dont le sujet sur le croisement des races humaines défraie de nouveau la chronique.

1932 Tourne son premier film *Nuit après nuit* avec George Raft.

1933 Forte du succès de *Diamond Lil*, la Paramount porte la pièce à l'écran, mais en change le nom pour *She done him wrong (Lady Lou)*. Le film obtient un succès magistral. Son film suivant, *Je ne suis pas un ange*, entraîne un renforcement de la censure au cinéma et l'application stricte du Production Code, jusque-là plus ou moins ignoré.

1934 Sous la pression exercée par le Production Code Office, la Paramount doit adoucir le scénario de *It Ain't No Sin* qui prend le titre de *Belle of the Nineties*, mais reste *Ce n'est pas un péché* en français.

1935 *Je veux être une lady* est le début de la fin des excès : la Paramount tente de changer l'image provocante de Mae West à l'écran.

1936 Incarne une danseuse repentie dans *Annie du Klondike*. Joue avec Randolph Scott dans *Go West Young Man*.

1937 *Fifi peau de pêche* crève les budgets, et fait un flop au box-office. Mae West est qualifiée de « poison du box-office » par les distributeurs.

1940 Sortie de *Mon petit poussin chéri* avec W. C. Fields.

1943 Apparaît dans quelques scènes de *Tropicana*.

1944 Première de la pièce *Catherine Was Great*. Mae West s'y croit la réincarnation de Catherine la Grande.

1948 Part en tournée à New York et à Londres avec *Diamond Lil*.

1954 Entame une série de tournées avec un spectacle de variétés où elle se produit entourée de culturistes.

1959 Publie son autobiographie, *Goodness Had Nothing to Do With It (La vertu n'est pas mon fort)*.

1961 Écrit la pièce *Sextette*.

1970 Retour au cinéma à 77 ans pour incarner Leticia Van Allen dans *Myra Breckinridge* de Gore Vidal.

1978 Joue Marlo Manners/Lady Barrington dans le film adapté de sa pièce *Sextette*.

22 novembre 1980 Mae West meurt d'une attaque d'apoplexie à Hollywood.

PORTRAIT FOR 'EVERY DAY'S A HOLIDAY' (1937)
Mae West: "Keep a diary, and someday it'll keep you." / Mae West: „Führe [‚keep'] Tagebuch, und eines Tages wird es Dich aufbewahren [‚keep']." / Mae West : « Tiens un journal et conserve-le précieusement, un jour c'est lui qui te conservera. »

4

FILMOGRAPHY

FILMOGRAFIE

FILMOGRAPHIE

Night after Night (fr. *Nuit après nuit*, 1932)
Maudie Triplett. Director/Regie/réalisation: Archie
Mayo.

**She Done Him Wrong (dt. *Sie tat ihm unrecht*,
fr. *Lady Lou*, 1933)**
Lady Lou. Director/Regie/réalisation: Lowell
Sherman.

**I'm No Angel (dt. *Ich bin kein Engel*, fr. *Je ne suis
pas un ange*, 1933)**
Tira. Director/Regie/réalisation: Wesley Ruggles.

**Belle of the Nineties (fr. *Ce n'est pas un péché*,
1934)**
Ruby Carter. Director/Regie/réalisation: Leo
McCarey.

Goin' to Town (fr. *Je veux être une lady*, 1935)
Cleo Borden. Director/Regie/réalisation:
Alexander Hall.

Klondike Annie (fr. *Annie du Klondike*, 1936)
Rose Carlton/Sister Annie/The Frisco Doll; Rose
Carlton/Schwester Annie/The Frisco Doll; Rose

Carlton/Sœur Annie/La Poupée de Frisco.
Director/Regie/réalisation: Raoul Walsh.

Go West Young Man (dt. *Auf in den Westen*, 1936)
Mavis Arden. Director/Regie/réalisation: Henry
Hathaway.

**Every Day's a Holiday (fr. *Fifi peau de pêche*,
1937)**
Peaches O' Day. Director/Regie/réalisation:
A. Edward Sutherland.

**My Little Chickadee (dt. *Mein kleiner Gockel*,
fr. *Mon petit poussin chéri*, 1940)**
Flower Belle Lee. Director/Regie/réalisation:
Edward F. Cline.

The Heat's On (fr. *Tropicana*, 1943)
Fay Lawrence. Director/Regie/réalisation: Gregory
Ratoff.

**Myra Breckinridge (dt. *Myra Breckinridge –
Mann oder Frau?*, 1970)**
Leticia Van Allen. Director/Regie/réalisation:
Michael Sarne.

Sextette (1978)
Marlo Manners/Lady Barrington.
Director/Regie/réalisation: Ken Hughes.

ADOLPH ZUKOR PRESENTS

MAE WEST

in

"Klondike Annie"

with VICTOR McLAGLEN

A PARAMOUNT PICTURE

BIBLIOGRAPHY

Curry, Ramona: *Mae West as Cultural Icon.* University of Minnesota, 1996.

Eells, George & Musgrove, Stanley: *Mae West: A Biography.* Robson, 1982.

Hamilton, Jack: 'Raquel Welch, Mae West Talk about Men, Morals and Myra Breckinridge.' *Look,* 24 March 1970.

Hamilton, Marybeth: *When I'm Bad, I'm Better: Mae West, Sex, and American Entertainment.* University of California, 1997.

Hanna, David: *Come Up and See Me Sometime: An Uncensored Biography of Mae West.* Belmont Tower, 1976.

Haskell, Molly: 'Mae West's Bawdy Spirit Spans the Gay Nineties.' *New York Times,* 15 August 1993, p. 14.

Jennings, Robert: 'Mae West: A Candid Interview with the Indestructible Queen of Vamp and Camp.' *Playboy,* January 1971.

Leider, Emily Wortis: *Becoming Mae West.* Da Capo, 2000.

Leonard, Maurice: *Mae West: Empress of Sex.* Carol, 1992.

Louvish, Simon: *Mae West: It Ain't No Sin.* Dunne, 2006.

Malachosky, Tim: *Mae West.* Empire, 1993.

Merryman, Richard: 'Mae West: A Cherished, Bemusing Masterpiece of Self-Preservation.' *Life,* 18 April 1969.

Roberston, Pamela: '"The Kinda Comedy That Imitates Me": Mae West's Identification with the Feminist Camp.' *Cinema Journal,* Winter 1993, pp. 57-72.

Thomas, Kevin: 'Mae West: At One with Her Image.' *Los Angeles Time Calendar,* 30 November 1980, p. 5.

Watts, Jill: Mae West: *An Icon in Black and White.* Oxford University, 2003.

West, Mae: *Goodness Had Nothing To Do with It.* Belvedere, 1959.

West, Mae: *Mae West on Health, Sex, and ESP.* W. H. Allen, 1975.

West, Mae: *The Wit and Wisdom of Mae West.* Berkley, 1977.

IMPRINT

© 2008 TASCHEN GmbH
Hohenzollernring 53, D-50672 Köln
www.taschen.com

Editor/Picture Research/Layout: Paul Duncan/Wordsmith Solutions
Editorial Coordination: Martin Holz and Katharina Krause, Cologne
Production Coordination: Nadia Najm and Horst Neuzner, Cologne
German Translation: Thomas J. Kinne, Nauheim
French Translation: France Varry, Cologne
Multilingual Production: www.arnaudbriand.com, Paris
Typeface Design: Sense /Net, Andy Disl and Birgit Reber, Cologne

Printed in Italy
ISBN 978-3-8228-2321-7

To stay informed about upcoming TASCHEN titles, please request our magazine at www.taschen.com /magazine or write to TASCHEN, Hohenzollernring 53, D-50672 Cologne, Germany, contact@taschen.com, Fax: +49-221-254919. We will be happy to send you a free copy of our magazine which is filled with information about all of our books.

All the photos in this book, except for those listed below, were supplied by The Kobal Collection.
British Film Institute Stills, Posters and Designs, London: pp. 25, 29, 60, 62, 73, 78, 89, 117, 128, 149.
Thanks to Dave Kent, Phil Moad and everybody at The Kobal Collection for their professionalism and kindness.